African American Voices

African American Voices

Volume I: A-J

Deborah Gillan Straub, *Editor*

AN IMPRINT OF GALE

African American Voices

Deborah Gillan Straub, *Editor*

Staff

Sonia Benson, *U·X·L Developmental Editor*
Carol DeKane Nagel, *U·X·L Managing Editor*
Thomas L. Romig, *U·X·L Publisher*

Shanna Heilveil, *Production Associate*
Evi Seoud, *Assistant Production Manager*
Mary Beth Trimper, *Production Director*

Michelle DiMercurio, *Art Director*
Cynthia Baldwin, *Product Design Manager*

 This book is printed on acid-free paper that meets the minimum requirements of American National Standard for Information Sciences—Permanence Paper for Printed Library Materials, ANSI Z39.48-1984.

Library of Congress Catalog Card Number 96-060859
Printed in the United States of America

ISBN 0-8103-9497-9 (Set)
ISBN 0-8103-9498-7 (Volume 1)
ISBN 0-8103-9499-5 (Volume 2)

10 9 8 7 6 5 4 3 2

U·X·L is an imprint of Gale Research

Advisory Board

Contents

Frederick Douglass

Volume 1: A-J

Volume 2: K-Z

Speech Topics
at a Glance

Bold numerals indicate volume numbers.
*For a more detailed listing of information
covered in these volumes, consult subject index.*

Women's rights

Reader's Guide

Sojourner Truth

Orators have played key roles throughout the history of the United States, where the spoken word has helped shape foreign and domestic policy ever since the nation began over 200 years ago. *African American Voices* collects in a single source excerpted speeches delivered by African American civil rights activists, religious leaders, educators, feminists, abolitionists, politicians, writers, and other key figures who have changed the course of history by speaking out on a variety of issues.

Voices selections range from the well-known, such as Martin Luther King, Jr.'s "I Have a Dream" and Sojourner Truth's "Ain't I a Woman?" speeches, to lesser-known and harder-to-find entries, such as Fannie Lou Hamer's chilling testimony to the Democratic National Convention about her efforts to register to vote in Mississippi in 1962. Many of the speeches address various issues of civil rights and activism, but others delve into the arts, health, or personal adventures. Major movements and milestones of African American history are presented by speakers who were the central players in these events.

It is not possible in this first edition of *African American Voices* to include all of the many prominent African American speakers who have shaped American history. The thirty-six speechmakers featured in these volumes were chosen by a knowledgable team of advisors from a list of well over 100 candidates suitable to this collection. Due to the unavailability of certain materials for publication, some important speeches of the last two centuries were regretfully omitted from the set. Despite these omissions, however, *Voices* provides a compelling array of African American thought and issues from the past two centuries. Entries were selected: a) to encompass a wide range of perspectives and backgrounds; b) to be engaging and accessible to students; and c) to provide first-hand—and often quite dramatic—insight into the key issues, events, and movements of African American history.

The entries in *African American Voices* are arranged alphabetically by speaker. Each begins with introductory material, providing a brief biography of the speaker and the historical context of the speech that follows. Informative sidebars expand on topics mentioned within the entries. A "Sources" section, directing the student to further readings on the speechmaker and his or her speeches, concludes each entry.

African American Voices also contains more than 90 black-and-white illustrations, a subject index, a listing of speeches by major topics, and a timeline. Words and phrases are defined in the lower margin of the page on which they appear.

Related Reference Sources

African American Almanac features a comprehensive range of historical and current information on African American life and culture. Organized into twenty-six subject chapters, including civil rights, the family, the arts, religion, business and labor, politics, music, sports, and education, the volumes contain more than three hundred black-and-white photographs and maps, a selected bibliography, and a subject index.

African American Biography profiles three hundred African Americans, both living and deceased, prominent in fields ranging from civil rights to athletics, politics to literature, entertainment to science, religion to the military. A black-and-white portrait accompanies each entry, and an index lists all profilees by field of endeavor.

African American Chronology explores significant social, political, economic, cultural, and educational milestones in black history. The chronologically arranged volumes span from 1492 to modern times and contain more than one hundred illustrations, extensive cross references, and a subject index.

Acknowledgments

The editor wishes to thank the following people who served as advisors on this project: Wil A. Linkugel, Professor of Communication Studies, University of Kansas, Lawrence, Kansas; Jeanette J. Smith, Regional Coordinator, Julia Davis Branch, St. Louis Public Library, St. Louis, Missouri; and Hilda K. Weisburg, Media Specialist, Sayreville War Memorial High School, Parlin, New Jersey.

Your Suggestions Are Welcome

The editor welcomes your comments and suggestions for future editions of *African American Voices*. Please write: The Editor, *African American Voices,* U•X•L, 835 Penobscot Building, Detroit, Michigan 48226-4094; call toll-free: 1-800-877-4253; or fax: (313) 961-6348.

Introduction

Traditions in African American Oratory

In the American tradition, there is a fundamental assumption that everyone has freedom of speech and the right to be heard in the public forum as guaranteed by the First Amendment to the Constitution. Imagine, then, the plight of some people in the United States who historically did not have freedom of speech—-African Americans. Because many of them were slaves from the seventeenth century until the Emancipation Proclamation freed them in 1863, they were not regarded as citizens. The U.S. Supreme Court reinforced this view in 1857 when it ruled that the Constitution had been written only for whites. Thus, as noncitizens without freedom of speech, blacks had to earn their "voice" in American society.

The roots of African American oratory can be traced back to oral African culture. In that environment, the human voice as well as drums were used to send messages, which another speaker or drummer would then respond to immedi-

Barbara Jordan

ately. Both the original message and the answer were often quite creative and reflected the African religious belief in the spirit world.

Once in America, Africans continued their creative ways of communicating. During the time of slavery, these methods included field chants, hollers, and music, much of which had double or hidden meanings. This prevented the masters from knowing the true message, lest the slaves be punished for plotting against them.

Free blacks in the North, on the other hand, enjoyed freedom of speech to a degree their enslaved brothers in the South never could. Thus it was in the North that we heard speakers such as Frederick Douglass and Sojourner Truth. While some of these orators (such as Truth) could neither read nor write, they nevertheless spoke with passion and, more often than not, with strong religious conviction.

Given her reputation as an eloquent and persuasive speaker, Sojourner Truth is, in fact, a good example of what has made so many African American orators effective—-their delivery, their style, and their voice tones. Truth spoke in deep, sonorous tones and projected a sense of confidence. There was also a spiritual quality in her oratory that is common among many African American orators, including Martin Luther King, Jr., and Jesse Jackson. They all give the impression that God is on their side, a practice known as mythication.

While Sojourner Truth most notably reflects the spiritualist tradition in African American oratory, she was unique in other ways that have implications for how we understand African American oratory today. First, she was a woman; second, she was African American; third, she was illiterate; and fourth, she was poor. As a black woman who spoke before white audiences, she recognized the social distance between women and men and between African American women and white women. For her, race, gender, and class were barriers to be surmounted. Addressing these very same barriers in more recent times are African American women orators such as Fannie Lou Hamer and Shirley Chisholm.

While the written public record provides us with a fair amount of information about what the early black orators in the North had to say in their speeches, it is only in recent years that technology has allowed us to capture fully the interactive dynamics that typically occur between African American orators and their audiences. When both the speaker and his or her audience are black (and occasionally in racially-mixed groups as well), there is almost always a spontaneous verbal exchange that takes place known as call-response. This lively verbal interplay is unique to the African American oratorical tradition and has roots that extend back to Africa.

Many of the early black orators were preachers, and their congregations continued the African tradition of providing an immediate response to the message. These responses were both verbal and nonverbal, such as saying "Amen," "Hallelujah," or "Thank you, Lord," or waving one's hands or standing and pointing toward the preacher. In this way, the congregation affirmed the messenger and created collective harmony with him or her and with the Holy Spirit.

Nowadays, call-response is a way of uniting the orator and the audience so that they become substantially one, making the communication between them circular rather than one-way. The orator does not consider the verbal and nonverbal feedback from the audience as an interruption. In fact, many African American orators solicit this kind of feedback to determine whether they are reaching their audience, asking questions such as "Is anybody with me?" or "Can I get a witness?" The audience gives an immediate response ("Right on," "Make it plain," "Go 'head," "Take your time"), and this in turn affirms the messenger and urges him or her on to greater oratorical heights.

In addition to documenting this colorful tradition, modern technology has also helped preserve the accuracy of black oratory. Accuracy is always a concern when orators speak without a written text or when the written text is not saved. For example, since Sojourner Truth did not write down her speeches, there is now some question as to the accuracy of the existing printed texts.

The importance of technology in establishing accuracy is also evident when oratory contains a combination of prepared written text and extemporaneous speech, as in Martin Luther King, Jr.'s "I Have a Dream" speech. Audio and video recordings allow us to pinpoint when King dispensed with the text and began to speak extemporaneously. Such recordings also play a vital role in helping us to hear the moving musical qualities of his voice.

While Sojourner Truth and Martin Luther King, Jr., represent the extremes of literacy in African American oratory, each was effective due to their mastery of language and their ethos. Like most African American orators, they felt an urgency to give voice to the needs of their people. Both spoke and gained recognition through the courage of their convictions.

Dorthy L. Pennington
Associate Professor
University of Kansas
Lawrence, Kansas

Suggested Readings

Boulware, Marcus H., *The Oratory of Negro Leaders, 1900—1968,* Negro Universities Press, 1969.

Foner, Philip S., editor, *The Voice of Black America: Major Speeches by Negroes in the United States, 1797–1971,* Simon & Schuster, 1972.

Gonzalez, Alberto, Marsha Houston, and Victoria Chen, editors, *Our Voices: Essays in Culture, Ethnicity and Communication,* Roxbury Publishing Company, 1994.

Halliburton, Warren J., *Historic Speeches of African Americans,* F. Watts, 1993.

Credits

Grateful acknowledgment is made to the following sources whose works appear in this volume. Every effort has been made to trace copyright, but If omissions have been made, please contact the publisher.

Carmichael, Stokely. From "Berkeley Speech" in *Stokely Speaks: Black Power Back to Pan-Africanism*. Random House, 1971. Reprinted by permission of the author.

Carson, Ben. From a speech delivered on June 27, 1994, at the Million Dollar Roundtable Convention in Dallas, Texas. Reprinted by permission of the author.

Cleaver, Eldridge. *The Black Panther,* v. 2, March 16, 1968, for "Political Struggle in America," by Eldridge Cleaver. Reprinted by permission of the author.

Dove, Rita. From a speech, "Who's Afraid of Poetry?," delivered on March 17, 1994, at the National Press Club. Reprinted by permission of the author.

Edelman, Marian Wright. From a speech delivered on June 9, 1994, at the Harvard University Medical School in Cambridge, Massachusetts. Reprinted by permission of the author. Marian Wright Edelman is the founder and president of the Children's Defense Fund.

Garvey, Marcus. From "The Principles of the Universal Negro Improvement Association" in *Philosophy and Opinions of Marcus Garvey.* Edited by Amy Jacques-Garvey. Arno Press, 1969. Reprinted by permission of the Literary Estate of the author.

Haley, Alex. From a speech delivered on January 30, 1992, at Hope College in Holland, Michigan. Reprinted by permission of the Estate of Alexander P. Haley.

Hamer, Fannie Lou. From a testimony delivered on August 22, 1964, before the Credentials Committee, in *Proceedings of the Democratic National Convention.* Democratic National Committee, 1964. Reprinted by permission of the publisher.

Jordan, Barbara. From "A New Beginning: A New Dedication," in *Representative American Speeches: 1976-1977.* Edited by Waldo W. Braden. H.W. Wilson, 1977. Copyright © 1977 by the H. W. Wilson Company. Reprinted by permission.

King, Martin Luther, Jr. From *A Testament of Hope: The Essential Writings of Martin Luther King, Jr.* Edited by James Melvin Washington. Harper & Row, Publishers, 1986. Copyright 1968 by The Estate of Martin Luther King, Jr. All rights reserved. Reprinted by arrangement with The Heirs of the Estate of Martin Luther King, Jr., c/o Writers House, Inc. as agent for the proprietor./From *Rhetoric of Racial Revolt,* by Roy L. Hill. Golden Bell Press, 1964. All rights reserved. Reprinted by arrangement with The Heirs of the Estate of Martin Luther King, Jr., c/o Writers House, Inc. as agent for the proprietor.

Malcolm X. From *Malcolm X Speaks: Selected Speeches and Statements.* Edited by George Breitman. Pathfinder, 1965. Copyright © 1965, 1989 by Betty Shabazz and Pathfinder Press. All rights reserved. Reprinted by permission.

Powell, Adam Clayton, Jr. From "Can There Be Any Good Thing Come Out of Nazareth?" in *Rhetoric of Black Revolution,* by Arthur L. Smith. Allyn and Bacon, 1969. Copyright © 1969 by Allyn and Bacon, Inc. All rights reserved. Reprinted by permission of Molefi Kete Asante, formerly Arthur L. Smith.

Prothrow-Stith, Deborah. *Christian Social Action,* v. 6, June, 1993. From a speech delivered in May 1993 to the United Methodist National Youth Ministry Organization, conference on youth and violence. Copyright © 1993 by the General Board of Church and Society of The United Methodist Church. Reprinted by permission of the publisher.

Young, Whitney M., Jr. *Vital Speeches of the Day,* v. XXXVI, September 15, 1970. Reprinted by permission of the publisher.

The photographs and illustrations appearing in African American Voices were received from the following sources:

Cover: Malcolm X. UPI/Corbis-Bettmann.

Timeline: Courtesy of the Library of Congress: xxvii (top), xxviii (bottom), xxix (bottom); **The Bettmann Archive/ Newsphotos, Inc.:** xxix (top), xxxi, xxxii (top), xxxii (bottom), xxxiii (bottom), xxxiv (top), xxxvi; **U.S. Army Photograph:** xxx; **AP/Wide World Photos:** xxxiii (top), xxxv.

The Bettmann Archive/Newsphotos, Inc.: pp. 6, 57, 78, 101, 139, 188, 207, 226, 235, 247, 349, 405; **AP/Wide World Photos:** pp. 8, 21, 35, 39, 46, 57, 59, 64, 69, 113, 119, 136, 147, 165, 195, 203, 215, 254, 259, 268, 275, 281, 287, 316, 321, 323; **U.S. Senate Historical Office:** p. 11; **Archive Photos, Inc.:** pp. 31, 231, 333, 359,: **Library of Congress:** pp. 17, 73, 81, 83, 103, 129, 241, 245, 303, 353, 356, 368, 376; **Chris Felver:** p. 87; **Children's Television Workshop:** p. 95; **The Granger Collection Ltd.:** pp. 119, 125, 309; **Lou Jones Studio:** p. 291; **University of Chicago Library:** p. 363; **U.S. Signal Corps. of National Archives:** p. 383; **National Urban League:** p. 399.

Timeline of Important African American Events

1776–1996

Boldface indicates speakers featured in these volumes

American Revolution to the Antislavery Movement, 1776–1860

1787 The Continental Congress bans slavery in the Northwest Territory.

1790 The first U.S. Naturalization Act allows only "free white persons" to become American citizens.

1791 The Bill of Rights (the first ten amendments to the Constitution) is ratified.

1793 Congress passes the first Fugitive Slave Law, making it a crime to hide an escaped slave.

1831 Nat Turner leads the most famous slave rebellion in American history. He is quickly captured and hanged.

1832 **Maria W. Miller Stewart** becomes the first American-born woman to give a public speech.

1843 At a national convention of black men held in Buffalo, New York, **Henry Highland Garnet** delivers a fiery speech urging slaves to revolt.

Nat Turner's capture

| 1776 | 1787 | | 1848 |
| Declaration of Independence | U.S. Constitution approved | 1812–1815 War of 1812 | Seneca Falls Convention for women's rights |

• • **1760** • • **1780** • • **1800** • • **1820** • • **1840** • •

Civil War poster urging blacks to join Union Army

1850 Congress approves the Compromise of 1850, which outlaws slave trade in Washington, D.C., allows it to continue throughout the South, and admits California to the Union as a free state.

1851 At a women's rights convention in Ohio, **Sojourner Truth** delivers her famous "Ain't I a Woman?" speech.

1852 **Frederick Douglass** delivers his powerful "Fourth of July Oration."

1857 The Supreme Court issues its *Dred Scott* decision, ruling that blacks cannot become citizens and have no rights under the Constitution, and that Congress has no power to prohibit slavery in any part of U.S. territory.

1859 White abolitionist John Brown raids the federal arsenal at Harpers Ferry, Virginia, to obtain weapons for slaves to use in a revolt against their masters. He is captured and executed.

Civil War and Reconstruction, 1861–1880

1862 Congress authorizes President Abraham Lincoln to accept blacks for service in the Union Army.

1863 President Lincoln issues the Emancipation Proclamation, freeing slaves in the states then at war against the Union.

1865 President Andrew Johnson announces his Reconstruction program for reorganizing and rebuilding the southern states.

Congress ratifies the 13th Amendment, which outlaws slavery in the United States.

1868 Congress ratifies the 14th Amendment, which recognizes blacks as American citizens with certain constitutional guarantees.

Abraham Lincoln at the first reading of the Emancipation Proclamation

1860
South Carolina secedes from the Union

1861
Confederate States of America form; Civil War begins

1865
Civil War ends; Reconstruction Era begins in South

1870 Congress ratifies the 15th Amendment, which states that no male American citizen can be denied the right to vote.

1875 Congress passes a civil rights bill (known as the Civil Rights Act of 1875) that outlaws discrimination in public places and on public transportation.

Blanche Kelso Bruce becomes the only black man to serve a full term in the Senate until the mid-twentieth century.

Pioneers in Civil Rights, 1881–1926

1881 Booker T. Washington opens the Tuskegee Institute in Alabama.

1883 The Supreme Court overturns the Civil Rights Act of 1875.

1892 **Ida B. Wells-Barnett** launches an anti-lynching campaign with a series of newspaper editorials that angrily expose the truth behind many of the attacks.

1895 **Booker T. Washington** delivers his "Atlanta Compromise" address.

1896 The Supreme Court issues its *Plessy v. Ferguson* decision upholding the "separate but equal" doctrine regarding the use of public places and public transportation by blacks.

1901 U.S. Representative **George H. White** of North Carolina delivers an impassioned farewell address to his colleagues upon leaving the House after two terms. More than twenty years pass before any other African Americans are elected to Congress.

1903 An essay in **W. E. B. Du Bois**'s book *The Souls of Black Folk* criticizes **Booker T. Washington,** touching off a bitter feud between the two leaders.

Booker T. Washington

W. E. B. Du Bois

1870		1886	
Women organize nationally to obtain vote	**1877** Reconstruction Era ends	Samuel Gompers forms the American Federation of Labor	**1898** Spanish-American War

Soldiers in World War II: 92nd (Negro) Division, Italy, 1944

1905 The Niagara Movement, the forerunner of the National Association for the Advancement of Colored People (NAACP), takes shape at a meeting in New York State. Many prominent black leaders attend, including **W. E. B. Du Bois** and **Ida B. Wells-Barnett**.

1909 The National Association for the Advancement of Colored People is founded. **W. E. B. Du Bois** serves as editor of its official publication, the *Crisis.*

1910 The National Urban League is founded.

1915 **Booker T. Washington** dies.

1916 **Marcus Garvey** establishes a branch of his Universal Negro Improvement Association in New York City.

1919 Led by **W. E. B. Du Bois**, the first Pan-African Congress meets in Paris, France.

Fighting Segregation, 1926–1960

1936 President Franklin D. Roosevelt appoints **Mary McLeod Bethune** to his unofficial "Black Cabinet." Among the president's other African American advisors is **Ralph Bunche.**

1941 President Roosevelt issues an executive order banning racial discrimination in the defense industry and in government training programs.

1944 **Adam Clayton Powell, Jr.,** is elected to the U.S. House of Representatives from a newly created district that includes the Harlem neighborhood of New York City, making him the first black congressman from the East.

1908
Henry Ford
unveils Model T

1914–1918
World War I

1929
Stock market crashes;
Great Depression
begins

1939–1945
World War II

• • **1905** • • **1915** • • **1925** • • **1935** • • **1945** • •

1948 President Harry S Truman issues an executive order calling for equality of treatment and opportunity for all Americans in the armed forces, thus officially ending segregation and discrimination in the military.

1950 **Ralph Bunche** becomes the first black to win the Nobel Peace Prize.

1952 **Malcolm X** is paroled from prison and soon becomes a minister in the Nation of Islam.

1954 The Supreme Court issues its landmark *Brown v. Board of Education of Topeka* decision overturning *Plessy v. Ferguson* and declaring racial segregation in public schools unconstitutional. Attorney **Thurgood Marshall** leads the NAACP legal team that argues the case before the justices.

1955 **Roy Wilkins** becomes executive secretary of the NAACP.

   Martin Luther King, Jr., launches a year-long bus boycott in Montgomery, Alabama, after Rosa Parks is arrested for refusing to give up her seat on a city bus to a white person.

1957 The Southern Christian Leadership Conference (SCLC) is cofounded by **Martin Luther King, Jr.**; he serves as its first president.

   Federal troops are sent to Little Rock, Arkansas, to stop local residents from interfering with the desegregation of a local public high school.

   Congress passes the Voting Rights Bill of 1957, the first major civil rights legislation since 1875.

1959 **Lorraine Hansberry**'s play *A Raisin in the Sun* becomes the first play by a black woman to open on Broadway.

Thurgood Marshall standing in front of Supreme Court, 1958

1945
Cold War begins between U.S. and Soviet Union

1950
Senator Joseph McCarthy begins crusade against communists

1950–1953
Korean War

1959
Fidel Castro leads successful revolution in Cuba

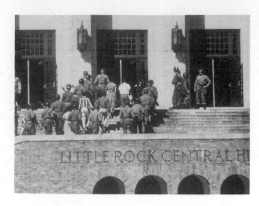

Federal troops escort black students during desegregation at Little Rock, Arkansas, High School

Civil Rights Activism, 1960–1965

1960 The Student Nonviolent Coordinating Committee (SNCC) is founded in the wake of civil rights sit-ins and demonstrations by young people throughout much of the South.

1961 **Whitney M. Young, Jr.,** becomes executive director of the National Urban League.

1963 **Martin Luther King, Jr.,** delivers his "I Have a Dream" speech to a crowd of more than 200,000 assembled at the Lincoln Memorial for the massive March on Washington civil rights demonstration.

1964 Congress ratifies the 24th Amendment, which outlaws the use of the poll tax to prevent people from voting.

Malcolm X drops out of the Nation of Islam to start his own movement.

Congress passes the Civil Rights Act of 1964, which prohibits discrimination in hiring and employment practices and paves the way for various affirmative action programs.

Martin Luther King, Jr., receives the Nobel Peace Prize.

Fannie Lou Hamer cofounds the Mississippi Freedom Democratic Party.

1965 **Malcolm X** is assassinated.

Led by **Martin Luther King, Jr.,** the SCLC launches a voter registration drive in Selma, Alabama, that escalates into a nationwide protest movement and ends in the famous "Freedom March" from Selma to Montgomery.

Martin Luther King, Jr., leads march from Selma to Montgomery, Alabama, 1965

1960
Militant student
movement begins
to organize

1963
President
John F. Kennedy
is assassinated

1965
United State sends
combat troops
to Vietnam

1965   Congress passes the Voting Rights Act of 1965, which prevents states from denying the right to vote to people unable or unwilling to pay a poll tax and to those unable to read or write English.

Racial disturbances erupt in the Watts ghetto of Los Angeles, California.

Burning buildings, Detroit riots, 1967

Black Power, 1966–1973

1966   **Stokely Carmichael** becomes head of the Student Nonviolent Coordinating Committee and promotes the concept of "black power."

Huey Newton and Bobby Seale establish the Black Panther Party. **Eldridge Cleaver** joins them and becomes a key spokesperson for the group.

1967   Race riots occur in Newark, New Jersey, Detroit, Michigan, and several other U.S. cities.

The Supreme Court rules unconstitutional all laws prohibiting interracial marriage.

Thurgood Marshall is sworn in as the first black justice of the Supreme Court.

1968   **Martin Luther King, Jr.,** is assassinated.

The new head of the SCLC, Ralph Abernathy, leads a group of blacks, whites, Native Americans, and Mexican Americans on a march to Washington, D.C., known as the "Poor People's Campaign."

The Kerner Commission releases the results of its investigation into the causes of the 1967 race riots, concluding that "white racism" was largely to blame.

Shirley Chisholm wins a seat in the House of Representatives, becoming the first black woman ever to serve in Congress.

Shirley Chisholm, 1972

1965	**1966**	**1968**
Demonstrators protest U.S. involvement in Vietnam War	National Organization for Women (NOW) is founded	Student protest demonstrations hit 221 U.S. campuses

• • **1965** • • **1966** • • **1967** • • **1968** • •

Jesse Jackson giving thumbs up to announce his candidacy for president, 1987

1969 The Supreme Court rules that public school districts must end racial segregation immediately.

1970 Racial violence erupts in school districts across the United States as court-ordered desegregation plans are implemented that continue through 1976.

1970 The Voting Rights Act of 1965 is extended until 1975.

1971 The Supreme Court rules that busing students to achieve racial desegregation is constitutional.

1972 **Shirley Chisholm** becomes the first black and the first woman to seek the Democratic nomination for president.

1973 **Marion Wright Edelman** establishes the Children's Defense Fund.

Milestones, 1974–1990

1974 After a series of hearings, the House Judiciary Committee—including **Barbara Jordan** of Texas—adopts three articles of impeachment against President Richard M. Nixon.

1975 The Voting Rights Act of 1965 is extended for an additional seven years.

1976 The Supreme Court rules that blacks and other minorities are entitled to retroactive job security.

Representative Barbara Jordan delivers a rousing keynote address at the Democratic National Convention.

1977 **Alex Haley** is awarded a special Pulitzer Prize for *Roots*.

1978 The Supreme Court issues its *Bakke* decision, declaring racial and ethnic quota systems in college admissions unconstitutional.

Bakke decision protest march

1969	1973	1974	1979–1981
U.S. astronaut Neil Armstrong walks on moon	United States signs cease-fire with North Vietnam	President Richard M. Nixon resigns after Watergate investigation	Fifty-two hostages are held at U.S. Embassy in Iran

1980   Miami, Florida, is the scene of the most serious racial disturbances in the country since the riots of the 1960s.

1986   The first national **Martin Luther King, Jr.,** holiday is celebrated.

Dr. **Ben Carson** performs the first successful separation of Siamese twins joined at the back of the head.

1988   Jesse Jackson places second behind Michael Dukakis in the delegate count to win the Democratic party's nomination for president of the United States.

1989   General **Colin Powell** becomes the first black chairman of the Joint Chiefs of Staff.

Clarence Thomas

The 1990s

1991   In Los Angeles, California, the beating of black motorist Rodney King by four white policemen is captured on videotape and broadcast on network news programs, sparking an international outcry.

Thurgood Marshall retires from the Supreme Court.

Clarence Thomas is confirmed for the Supreme Court after controversial hearings during which University of Oklahoma law professor Anita Hill accuses him of sexual harassment.

1992   Racial violence erupts in Los Angeles, California, after four white police officers are acquitted in the beating of black motorist Rodney King.

Carol Moseley-Braun of Illinois becomes the first black woman elected to the U.S. Senate.

1993   **Rita Dove** is named poet laureate of the United States.

Toni Morrison becomes the first black woman to win the Nobel Prize for literature.

1981
Sandra Day O'Connor becomes the first woman member of the Supreme Court

1989
German reunification; Berlin Wall falls

1990–1991
Persian Gulf War

1991
Dissolution of the Soviet Union; Cold War ends

• • **1980** • • **1983** • • **1985** • • **1988** • • **1990** • • **1993** • •

*The Million Man March,
Washington, D.C., 1995*

1994 In the mid-term elections, the Republicans regain majorities in both the House of Representatives and the Senate for the first time in forty years.

1995 Republicans in Congress begin work on the reforms and budget cuts proposed in their "Contract with America." Opponents such as Jesse Jackson and **Marian Wright Edelman** condemn the "Contract" as devastating to the poor, children, and the elderly.

In two separate decisions written by Justice **Clarence Thomas,** the Supreme Court comes out in favor of sharply limiting federal affirmative-action programs and court-ordered school integration efforts.

The Supreme Court declares unconstitutional the practice of using race as the major factor in drawing legislative districts.

Led by Nation of Islam leader Louis Farrakhan and former NAACP executive director Benjamin Chavis, the "Million Man March" attracts hundreds of thousands of African American men to Washington, D.C., to promote black self-help and self-discipline.

Retired General **Colin Powell** announces that he will not run for president in 1996.

1996 The Children's Defense Fund and **Marian Wright Edelman** organize a "Stand for Children" march and rally on June 1 in Washington, D.C.

1994	1995	1996
North American Free Trade Agreement (NAFTA) goes into effect	Bombing of Federal Building in Tulsa, Oklahoma	Israeli Prime Minister Yitzhak Rabin is assassinated

African American Voices

Mary McLeod Bethune

1875–1955
Educator and civil rights activist

Mary McLeod Bethune was without a doubt one of the best-known and most respected women of the twentieth century. She grew up during a time of great desperation and hardship for African Americans, and she personally had to overcome poverty and prejudice to make her dreams become reality. A very popular lecturer before audiences of all sizes in towns and cities across the United States, Bethune conveyed a sense of dignity, warmth, and deep spirituality to her listeners, while she powerfully advanced her cause of racial harmony and equal opportunity.

Early Life

A native of South Carolina, Bethune was the fifteenth of seventeen children. Her parents were former slaves who farmed a small plot of land they had bought from their former owners after the Civil War. Young Mary was not allowed to attend the local public schools on account of her race, so she received her elementary, secondary, and early

"IF OUR PEOPLE ARE TO FIGHT THEIR WAY UP OUT OF BONDAGE WE MUST ARM THEM WITH THE SWORD AND THE SHIELD AND THE BUCKLER OF PRIDE—BELIEF IN THEMSELVES AND THEIR POSSIBILITIES, BASED UPON A SURE KNOWLEDGE OF THE ACHIEVEMENTS OF THE PAST."

college education at mission schools run by the Presbyterian Church. She then continued her studies at Chicago's Moody Bible Institute. Bethune wanted very much to become a missionary, but her application was rejected in 1895 on the grounds that she was only twenty and therefore too young. So she began teaching instead at several small schools throughout the South before finally settling in Daytona Beach, Florida, in 1904.

Opens Her Own School

In Daytona Beach, Bethune decided to open a school for the children of black construction workers working on a nearby railroad project. The job was a difficult one at best. Most of the families she approached lived in terrible poverty and faced a constant battle with crime and the threat of racial violence. Not very many parents were interested in listening to her plans for starting a school. But Bethune kept pushing her idea and soon opened the Daytona Normal and Industrial School for Negro Girls.

The school's first home was a ramshackle old building that Bethune herself scrubbed and repaired. She earned the money to pay for some of these efforts by making pies, ice cream, and fried fish that she then sold to construction crews. Furniture and supplies were either homemade or pulled from the garbage outside some of the city's resort hotels. Bethune also went door to door asking for donations of all kinds from individuals, churches, clubs, and other groups.

Classes at the Daytona School emphasized practical studies—reading, writing, and arithmetic and vocational skills such as cooking and sewing. Enrollment grew quickly over the next few years, and in 1907 Bethune set her sights on expanding. First, she purchased thirty-two acres of neighboring swamp and dump property that nobody else wanted. Then, with secondhand material and labor provided by the fathers of some of her students (in exchange for tuition fees), she cleaned up the land and built several new buildings. Enrollment continued to grow at a slow but steady pace, and in 1928 the Daytona School merged with the Cookman Institute, a Jacksonville-based boys' school. The new institution then became known as Bethune-Cookman College.

The Presidential Cabinet

The cabinet of the president of the United States consists of the men and women who officially advise the chief executive on major policies and programs. Current members of the cabinet include the heads of the departments of State, Treasury, Defense, Health and Human Services, Energy, Education, Housing and Urban Development, Transportation, Agriculture, Interior, Commerce and Labor, Justice, and Veterans Affairs. The president may also consult with many other people outside the government on an unofficial or informal basis. This unofficial group of advisers is often referred to as the "kitchen cabinet."

During the 1930s and early 1940s, a group of African American leaders called the "Black Cabinet" served as unofficial advisers to President Franklin D. Roosevelt. Mary McLeod Bethune was one of the organizers of the group, which included other educators as well as professionals in fields such as economics and law. They kept the president informed on issues of importance to African Americans and other minorities. Some members of the Black Cabinet (such as Bethune) eventually held official government posts.

Takes on New Responsibilities in Nation's Capital

Meanwhile, Bethune's vision and determination to make her school succeed had earned her fame and respect throughout the country. As a result, she ended up spending most of the 1930s in Washington, D.C., where she became involved in a wide variety of activities. A member of the unofficial "Black Cabinet" of President Franklin Roosevelt, Bethune served as one of his advisors on minority affairs and also worked closely with his wife, Eleanor, on a number of issues of interest to both women. In 1936, she took on an official government role as director of Negro affairs for the National Youth Administration. In this job, she supervised the development of recreational and vocational programs for young African Americans. During this period, Bethune established and headed the National Council of Negro Women and worked with the National Association for the Advancement of Colored People (NAACP), the National Urban League, and the Association for the Study of Negro Life and History. In addition, she was much in demand as a speaker and as a contributor to magazines and newspapers.

Bethune's views on the racial situation in America in many ways bridged the gap between the conservatism of

Booker T. Washington *(see entry) and the radicalism of* *W. E. B. Du Bois* *(see entry), two black leaders of the early twentieth century. Like Washington, Bethune believed that African Americans should obtain the job skills that would bring them economic success. But she disagreed with him on the subject of obtaining civil and social equality. He thought that blacks should wait patiently for whites to grant them their rights at some distant and undetermined future date. Du Bois completely rejected that idea and demanded immediate and total equality for blacks. Bethune felt that both problems—achieving economic success as well as civil and social equality—should be tackled at once.*

Bethune was a skillful diplomat during her years in the national spotlight. She learned to deal with whites on their terms but remained true to her own beliefs, which were somewhat more militant than she usually revealed in public to all-white or mixed-race audiences. In speaking to all-black audiences, however, she took a stronger position.

The following speech is an example of one of her talks before a black audience. It was delivered October 31, 1937, in Washington, D.C., at the annual meeting of the Association for the Study of Negro Life and History (ASNLH). Founded by Professor Carter G. Woodson in 1915, the ASNLH was determined to increase the public's awareness of the true role of blacks in American history. Bethune was very active in the group and served for a time as its president.

In her speech that day, Bethune challenged her listeners to do their best to give young blacks a sense of pride in their race. This was a common theme in her addresses, as was the sense of drama she created to help make her point and establish a bond with her audience. An excerpt from her remarks is reprinted here from the ASNLH's Journal of Negro History, *Volume 23, published in 1938.*

John Vandercook's *Black Majesty* tells the dramatic story of Jean Christophe, the black emperor of Haiti, and how he molded his empire with his bare hands out of the rugged cliffs and the unchained slaves of his native land. One night, in the midst of his Herculean struggles, Sir Home, his English adviser, accused him of building too fast and working his subjects like slaves until they were discontent.... "For a long moment Christophe was silent.... When he spoke, his full rich voice seemed suddenly old.

"You do not understand...."

He stopped again, seemed to be struggling for words. Then he went on:

"My race is as old as yours. In Africa, they tell me, there are as many blacks as there are white men in Europe. In Saint Domingue, before we drove the French out, there were a hundred Negroes to every master. But we were your slaves. Except in Haiti, nowhere in the world have we resisted you. We have suffered, we have grown dull, and, like cattle under a whip, we have obeyed. Why? Because we have no pride! And we have no pride because we have nothing to remember. Listen!"

He lifted his hand. From somewhere behind them was coming a faint sound of drumming, a monotonous, weird melody that seemed to be born of the heart of the dark, rearing hills, that rose and fell and ran in pallid echoes under the moon. The King went on.

"It is a drum, Sir Home. Somewhere my people are dancing. It is almost all we have. The drum, laughter, love for one another, and our share of courage. But we have nothing white men can understand. You despise our dreams and kill the snakes and break the little sticks you think are our gods. Perhaps if we had something we could show you, if we had something we could show ourselves, you would respect us and we might respect ourselves.

"If we had even the names of our great men! If we could lay our hands"—he thrust his out—"on things we've made, monuments and towers and palaces, we might find our strength, gentlemen. While I live I shall try to build that pride we need, and build in terms white men as well as black can understand! I am thinking of the future, not of now. I will teach pride if my teaching breaks every back in my kingdom."

peonage: the state of being legally obligated to someone to work off debts.

Today I would salute in homage that wise old emperor. I bring you again his vibrant message. Our people cry out all around us like children lost in the wilderness. Hemmed in by a careless world, we are losing our homes and our farms and our jobs. We see vast numbers of us on the land sunk into the degradation of **peonage** and virtual slavery. In the cities, our workers are barred from the unions, forced to "scab" and often to fight with their very lives for work. About us cling the ever-tightening tentacles of poor wages, economic insecurity, sordid homes, labor by women and children, broken homes, ill health, delinquency and crime. Our children are choked by denied opportunity for health, for education, for work, for recreation, and thwarted with their ideals and ambitions still a-borning. We are scorned of men; they spit in our faces and laugh. We cry out in this awesome darkness. Like a clarion call, I invoke today again the booming voice of Jean Christophe—

"If we had something we could show you, if we had something we could show ourselves, you would respect us and we might respect ourselves. If we had even the names of our great men! If we could lay our hands on things we've made, monuments and towers and palaces, we might find our strength, gentlemen...."

If our people are to fight their way up out of bondage we must arm them with the sword and the shield and the buckler of pride—belief in themselves and their possibilities, based upon a sure knowledge of the achievements of the past. That knowledge and that pride we must give them "if it breaks every back in the kingdom."

Through the scientific investigation and objective presentation of the facts of our history and our achievement to ourselves and to all men, our Association for the Study of Negro Life and History serves to tear the veil from our eyes and allow us to see clearly and in true perspective our rightful place among all men. Through accurate research and investigation, we serve so to supplement, correct, re-orient and annotate the story of world progress as to enhance the standing of our group in the eyes of all men. In the one hand, we bring pride to our own; in the other, we bear respect from the others.

We must tell the story with continually accruing detail from the cradle to the grave. From the mother's knee and the fireside of the home, through the nursery, the kindergarten and the grade school, high school, college and university, through the technical journals, studies and bulletins of the Association, through newspaper, storybook and pictures, we must tell the thrilling story. When they learn the fairy tales of mythical king and queen and princess, we must let them hear,

Mary M. Bethune Memorial, Washington, D. C.

too, of the pharaohs and African kings and the brilliant pageantry of the Valley of the Nile; when they learn of Caesar and his legions, we must teach them of Hannibal and his Africans; when they learn of [William] Shakespeare and [German poet Johann Wolfgang von] Goethe, we must teach them of [Russian poet Aleksandr] Pushkin and Dumas. When they read of [Christopher] Columbus, we must introduce the Africans who touched the shores of America before Europeans emerged from savagery; when they are thrilled by [American Revolution hero] Nathan Hale, baring his breast and crying: "I have but one life to give for my country," we must make their hearts leap to see Crispus Attucks [an American patriot who was killed by the British in the "Boston Massacre" in 1770] stand and fall for liberty on Boston Common with the red blood of freedom streaming down his breast. With the *Tragic Era* we give them *Black Reconstruction;* with [inventor Thomas] Edison, we give them [inventor] Jan Matzeliger; with John Dewey, we place Booker T. Washington; above the folk music of the cowboy and the hillbilly, we place the spiritual and the "blues"; when they boast of [artist] Maxfield Parrish, we show them [artist] E. Simms Campbell. Whatever man has done, we have done—and often, better. As we tell this story, as we present to the world the facts, our pride in racial achievement grows, and our respect in the eyes of all men heightens.

Certainly, too, it is our task to make plain to ourselves the great story of our rise in America from "less than the dust" to the heights of sound achievement.... It is the duty of our Association to tell the glorious story of our past and of our marvelous achievement in American life over almost insuperable obstacles.

From this history, our youth will gain confidence, self-reliance and courage. We shall thereby raise their mental horizon and give them a base from which to reach out higher and higher into the realm of achievement. And as we look about us today, we know that they must have this courage and self-reliance. We are beset on every side with heart-rending and fearsome difficulties.

Recently, in outlining to the president of the United States the position of the Negro in America, I saw fit to put it this way: "The great masses of Negro workers are depressed and unprotected in the lowest levels of agriculture and domestic service while black workers in industry are generally barred from the unions and grossly discriminated against. The housing and living conditions of the Negro masses are sordid and unhealthy; they live in constant terror of the mob, generally shorn of their constitutionally guaranteed right of suffrage, and humiliated by the denial of civil liberties. The great masses of Negro youth are offered only one-fifteenth the educational opportunity of the average American child."

These things also we must tell them, accurately, realistically and factually. The situation we face must be defined, reflected and evaluated. Then, armed with the pride and courage of his glorious tradition, conscious of his positive contribution to American life, and enabled to face clear-eyed and unabashed the actual situation before him, the Negro may gird his loins and go forth to battle to return "with their shields or on them." And so today I charge our Association for the Study of Negro Life and History to carry forward its great mission to arm us with the facts so that we may face the future with clear eyes and a sure vision. Our Association may say again with Emperor Jean Christophe: "While I live I shall try to build that pride we need, and build in terms white men as well as black can understand! I am thinking of the future, not of now. I will teach pride if my teaching breaks every back in my Kingdom."

Sources

Books

Anderson, Judith, editor, *Outspoken Women: Speeches by American Women Reformers, 1635–1935*, Kendall/Hunt Publishing Company, 1984.

Boulware, Marcus H., *The Oratory of Negro Leaders: 1900–1968,* Negro Universities Press, 1969.

Halasa, Malu, *Mary McLeod Bethune,* Chelsea House, 1989.

Holt, Rackham, *Mary McLeod Bethune,* Doubleday, 1964.

Lerner, Gerda, editor, *Black Women in White America: A Documentary History,* Pantheon Books, 1972.

Periodicals

Ebony, "My Last Will and Testament," August 1955, reprinted, November 1990, pp. 128-134.

Journal of Negro History, "Clarifying Our Vision with the Facts," Volume 23, 1938, pp. 10-15; "The Negro in Retrospect and Prospect," Volume 35, 1950, pp. 9-19; "Mary McLeod Bethune," October 1955, pp. 393-395.

Newsweek, "Faith in a Swampland," May 30, 1955, p. 47.

New York Times, May 19, 1955, p. 29.

Time, "Matriarch," July 22, 1946, p. 55.

Blanche Kelso Bruce

1841–1898

Educator, businessman, and politician

As the first African American to serve a full six-year term as a United States senator, Blanche Kelso Bruce holds a special place in history. (It was not until the middle of the twentieth century that another black accomplished the same feat—Edward Brooke of Massachusetts, who was elected to two terms in the U.S. Senate during the 1960s and 1970s.) During much of his time in office, Bruce was the only black in Congress, and he willingly assumed the role of spokesperson for his race and for other races he felt had been mistreated by the laws and customs of an indifferent and sometimes hostile nation.

Early Life

The youngest of eleven children, Bruce was the son of a Virginia slave woman named Polly. His father was an unknown white man, probably his mother's master, Pettus Perkinson. Bruce's last name came from the man who had owned his mother and ten brothers and sisters before he was born.

"WE WANT PEACE AND GOOD ORDER AT THE SOUTH; BUT IT CAN ONLY COME BY THE FULLEST RECOGNITION OF THE RIGHTS OF ALL CLASSES. THE OPPOSITION MUST CONCEDE THE NECESSITY OF CHANGE...."

During the late 1840s, Perkinson moved his family and his slaves back and forth across several southern states. Eventually, they all settled in Missouri. There, Bruce began working as a personal servant to his master's son and was allowed to receive a basic education from the son's private tutor. Later, Bruce labored as a field hand, a factory worker, and a printer's apprentice.

Escapes from Slavery

*During the early days of the Civil War, Bruce escaped to freedom in Lawrence, Kansas. There he opened the state's first elementary school for blacks and continued his own education under the guidance of a minister. After Missouri's slaves were freed in January 1865, he returned home and briefly resumed his career as a schoolteacher and a printer's apprentice before heading off to Ohio to attend Oberlin College. His money only lasted a few months, however, so he was soon forced to take a job as a **porter** on a riverboat.*

In 1869, having heard that the state of Mississippi had much to offer an ambitious young man such as himself, Bruce headed south to make his fortune. He quickly became involved in politics, serving first as supervisor of elections in Tallahatchie County and then as sergeant-at-arms in the state senate, sheriff and tax assessor in Bolivar County, and superintendent of education and alderman in the town of Floreyville. He also purchased a plantation and soon became a wealthy and respected businessman.

Elected to the United States Senate

In 1874, the Mississippi legislature elected Bruce to the United States Senate. He was the second black Mississippian to serve in that position—the first was Hiram Revels, who was in office for just over a year, from 1870 to 1871. Bruce's first appearance in the Senate chamber was a highly dramatic and much-publicized moment. His fellow Mississippi senator, a white man, refused to honor custom by escorting him to the swearing-in ceremony. Instead, Senator Roscoe Conkling of New York stepped forward, took the black legislator by the hand, and led him to the front of the room.

Bruce joined the Senate at a critical time in American history. The Republican-led reform movement that had domi-

porter: a person who carries baggage.

The Reconstruction Era

For a period of about ten years after the Civil War ended in 1865, the U.S. government—led by reform-minded Republicans—adopted a series of measures intended to help rebuild the defeated Confederate states and prepare them to rejoin the Union. Under the terms of this Reconstruction program, all of the Southern states were required to write new constitutions, allow black men to vote, elect new state officials, and ratify, or approve, the Fourteenth Amendment, which recognized blacks as U.S. citizens and guaranteed their constitutional rights.

These requirements led to many battles between the so-called "Radical Republicans" and Southern Democrats. But they also paved the way for a number of African Americans to run for political office at the local, state, and national level. From 1865 until 1877, for example, there were four black lieutenant governors (one of whom went on to serve briefly as acting governor), two U.S. senators, and twenty U.S. congressmen. There were also a number of other government officials, including three secretaries of state, a state supreme court justice, and two state treasurers.

Beginning around 1877, however, the influence of the Radical Republicans began to fade, and along with it the support for Reconstruction programs also disappeared. Southern Democrats wasted little time regaining control of state governments. With little or no interference from the federal government, they passed many discriminatory laws that legalized segregation and kept blacks from voting. Before long, African Americans in the South found themselves living under conditions that were nearly as bad as those they had endured under slavery.

nated national and local politics since the end of the Civil War (the Reconstruction Era; see box) was running out of steam, especially in the South. In the elections of 1875, Bruce's own home state of Mississippi was the scene of especially bold examples of **fraud** and **intimidation** as white Democrats tried to push aside the mostly black Republicans and gain control of the state. Their underhanded ways sparked outrage and controversy in the halls of Congress.

Finally, Senator Oliver Morton of Indiana, acting on behalf of a Michigan senator, proposed that a special committee be formed to investigate election practices in Mississippi. On March 31, 1876, Bruce stood before his colleagues in the Senate and explained the seriousness of the problem and the need to take immediate action on Morton's idea. An excerpt of his speech is reprinted here from

fraud: cheating, deception, trickery.

intimidation: actions intended to frighten or threaten.

the Congressional Record, *44th Congress, 1st Session, U.S. Government Printing Office, 1876, pp. 2101-2104.*

66

The close of the war found four millions of freed-men, without homes or property, charged with the duty of self-support and with the oversight of their personal freedom, yet without civil and political rights! The problem presented by this condition of things was one of the gravest that has ever been submitted to the American people.... [But] the practical sense of the American people definitely settled this delicate and difficult question....

We began our political career under the disadvantages of the inexperience in public affairs that generations of enforced bondage had entailed upon our race. We suffered also from the vicious leadership of some of the men whom our necessities forced us temporarily to accept. Consider further that the states of the South, where we were supposed to control by our majorities, were in an impoverished and semi-revolutionary condition—society demoralized, the industries of the country **prostrated,** the people sore, morbid, and sometimes turbulent, and no healthy controlling public opinion either existent or possible....

Despite the difficulties and drawbacks suggested, the constitutions formed under colored majorities, whatever their defects may be, were improvements on the instruments they were designed to supersede; and the statutes framed, though necessarily defective because of the crude and varying social and industrial conditions upon which they were based, were more in harmony with the spirit of the age and the genius of our free institutions than the obsolete laws that they **supplanted.** Nor is there just or any sufficient grounds upon which to charge an oppressive administration of the laws....

If it can be shown that we have used the ballot either to **abridge** the rights of our fellow citizens or to oppress them; if it shall appear that we have ever used our newly acquired power as a sword of attack and not as a shield of defense, then we may with some show of **propriety** be charged with incapacity, dishonesty, or tyranny. But, even then, I submit that the corrective is in the hands of the people, and not of a

prostrated: helpless, worn out.

supplanted: replaced.

abridge: decrease.

propriety: correctness.

favored class, and the remedy is in the honest exercise of the ballot, and not in fraud and violence.

Mr. President, do not misunderstand me; I do not hold that all the white people of the state of Mississippi aided and abetted the white-league organizations. There is in Mississippi a large and respectable element among the opposition who are not only honest in their recognition of the political rights of the colored citizen and **deprecate** the fraud and violence through which those rights have been assailed, but who would be glad to see the color line in politics abandoned and goodwill obtain and govern among all classes of her people. But the fact is to be regretted that this better class of citizens in many parts of the state is dominated by a turbulent and violent element of the opposition, known as the White League—a ferocious minority—and has thus far proved powerless to prevent the recurrence of the outrages it deprecates and deplores.

The uses of this investigation are various. It will be important in suggesting such action as may be found necessary not only to correct and repair the wrongs perpetrated, but to prevent their recurrence. But I will venture to assert that the investigation will be most beneficial in this, that it will largely contribute to the formation of a public sentiment that, while it restrains the vicious in their attacks upon the rights of the loyal, law-abiding voters of the South, will so energize

deprecate: disapprove of, condemn.

the laws as to secure **condign** punishment to wrongdoers, and give a security to all classes, which will effectively and abundantly produce the mutual goodwill and confidence that constitute the foundations of the public prosperity.

We want peace and good order [in] the South; but it can only come by the fullest recognition of the rights of all classes. The opposition must concede the necessity of change, not only in the temper but in the philosophy of their party organization and management. The sober American judgment must obtain in the South as elsewhere in the Republic, that the only distinctions upon which parties can be safely organized and in harmony with our institutions are differences of opinions relative to principles and policy of government, and that differences of religion, nationality, or race can neither with safety nor propriety be permitted for a moment to enter into the party contests of the day....

We simply demand the practical recognition of the rights given us in the Constitution and laws, and ask from our white fellow citizens only the consideration and fairness that we so willingly extend to them. Let them generally realize and concede that citizenship imports to us what it does to them, no more and no less, and impress the colored people that a party defeat does not imperil their political franchise. Let them cease their attempts to coerce our political cooperation, and invite and secure it by a policy so fair and just as to commend itself to our judgment, and resort to no motive or measure to control us that self-respect would preclude their applying to themselves. When we can entertain opinions and select party affiliations without proscription, and cast our ballots as other citizens and without jeopardy to person or privilege, we can safely afford to be governed by the considerations that ordinarily determine the political action of American citizens. But we must be guaranteed in the unproscribed exercise of our honest convictions and be absolutely, from within or without, protected in the use of our ballot before we can either wisely or safely divide our vote. In union, not division, is strength....

It has been suggested, as the popular sentiment of the country, that the colored citizens must no longer expect special legislation for their benefit, nor exceptional interference

condign: worthy.

Blanche Kelso Bruce

by the national government for their protection. If this is true, if such is the judgment relative to our demands and needs, I venture to offset the suggestion, so far as it may be used as reason for a denial of the protection we seek, by the statement of another and more prevalent popular conviction. Back of this, and underlying the foundations of the Republic itself, there lies deep in the breasts of the patriotic millions of the country the conviction that the laws must be enforced, and life, liberty, and property must, alike to all for all, be protected. But I allege that we do not seek special action in our behalf, except to meet special danger, and only then such as all classes of citizens are entitled to receive under the Constitution. We do not ask the enactment of new laws, but only the enforcement of those that already exist....

Poster attacking the Freedman's Bureau, illustrating the exploitation of racism in party politics that Bruce strongly opposed.

Blanche Kelso Bruce   17

I have felt, as the only representative of my race in the Senate of the United States, that I was placed, in some sort, upon the defensive, and I have consequently endeavored to show how aggravated and inexcusable were the wrongs worked upon us, and have sought to **vindicate** our title to both the respect and goodwill of the just people of the nation. The gravity of the issues involved has demanded great plainness of speech from me. But I have endeavored to present my views to the Senate with the moderation and deference inspired by the recollection that both my race and myself were once **bondsmen,** and are today debtors largely to the love and justice of a great people for the enjoyment of our personal and political liberty. While my **antecedents** and surroundings suggest modesty, there are some considerations that justify frankness, and even boldness of speech.

Mr. President, I represent, in an important sense, the interest of nearly a million of voters, constituting a new, hopeful, permanent, and influential political element, and large enough to affect in critical periods the fortunes of this great Republic; and the public safety and common **weal** alike demand that the integrity of this element should be preserved and its character improved....

I have confidence, not only in my country and her institutions, but in the endurance, capacity and destiny of my people. We will, as opportunity offers and ability serves, seek our places, sometimes in the field of letters, arts, science, and the professions. More frequently mechanical pursuits will attract and elicit our efforts; more still of my people will find employment and livelihood as the cultivators of the soil. The bulk of this people—by surroundings, habits, adaptation, and choice—will continue to find their homes in the South.... We will there, probably of our own **volition** and more abundantly than in the past, produce the great staples that will contribute to the basis of foreign exchange, aid in giving the nation a balance of trade, and minister to the wants and comforts and build up the prosperity of the whole land. Whatever our ultimate position in the **composite** civilization of the Republic and whatever varying fortunes attend our career, we will not forget our instincts for freedom nor our love of country. Guided and guarded by a beneficent Providence, and living under the genial influence of liberal institutions, we have

vindicate: justify.

bondsmen: slaves.

antecedents: ancestors, family background.

weal: well-being.

volition: choice, free will.

composite: combined, blended.

no apprehensions that we shall fail from the land from **attrition** with other races, or ignobly disappear from either the politics or industries of the country.

Mr. President, allow me here to say that, although many of us are uneducated in the schools, we are informed and advised as to our duties to the government, our state, and ourselves. Without class prejudice or animosities, with obedience to authority, as the lesson and love of peace and order as the passion of our lives, with scrupulous respect for the rights of others, and with the hopefulness of political youth, we are determined that the great government that gave us liberty, and rendered its gift valuable by giving us the ballot, shall not find us wanting in a sufficient response to any demand that humanity or patriotism may make upon us; and we ask such action as will not only protect us in the enjoyment of our constitutional rights, but will preserve the integrity of our republican institutions.

Throughout his entire Senate career, Bruce took vigorous action on behalf of African Americans not just on voting rights but in other areas as well. For example, he introduced legislation demanding that the armed forces be desegregated and supported equal treatment for black members of the military. In addition, he was a strong **advocate** *of providing industrial education to African Americans. He also voted in favor of giving financial help to Southern blacks who wanted to migrate west during the so-called "Great Exodus" of the late 1870s.*

As chairman of a special Senate investigating committee, Bruce played a key role in straightening out the tangled affairs of the mismanaged Freedmen's Bank after it went bankrupt in 1874. The Freedmen's Bank (or Freedmen's Savings and Trust Company) was established by Congress immediately after the Civil War to encourage former slaves to save and manage their money. Eager depositors helped the bank grow quickly; by 1872 it had expanded to more than thirty offices across the South as well as in New York City and Philadephia. Before long, however, it was on shaky financial ground due to reckless management practices and

attrition: friction.
advocate: promoter, supporter.

*widespread corruption. By the time **Frederick Douglass** (see entry) was named president of the Freedmen's Bank in March 1874 with orders to straighten out the mess, it was near collapse. The bank closed three months later, and for several years it appeared that none of the depositors would ever see any of their money again. But Bruce worked tirelessly to persuade the government that it had an obligation to the people who had trusted their life savings to the Freedmen's Bank. Eventually, thanks to his efforts, the depositors received three-fifths of their money back.*

*Bruce did not just help members of his own race, however. He often stood up for other people he thought were treated unfairly by the laws and customs of the nation. In 1878, for instance, he voted against a bill known as the Chinese Exclusion Act that proposed banning Chinese laborers and their families from entering the United States. (The measure passed and was not repealed until 1943.) Bruce also criticized what he called the government's "selfish" policy toward Native Americans. He felt it was slowly but surely leading to their destruction. Instead, he favored a strategy that encouraged them to **assimilate** into the mainstream culture.*

Sources

Books

Christopher, Maurine, *America's Black Congressmen,* Crowell, 1971.

Congressional Record, 44th Congress, 1st Session, U.S. Government Printing Office, 1876, pp. 2101-2104; 46th Congress, 2nd Session, U.S. Government Printing Office, 1880, pp. 2195-2196.

Periodicals

Journal of Negro History, "A Negro Senator," July 1922, pp. 243-256.

Negro History Bulletin, "Three Negro Senators of the United States: Hiram R. Revels, Blanche K. Bruce, and Edward W. Brooke," January 1967, pp. 4-5, 12.

assimilate: become absorbed into, become part of.

Ralph Bunche

1904–1971
Diplomat

In 1950, Ralph Bunche became the first African American ever awarded the Nobel Peace Prize. Thanks to his efforts as a negotiator for the United Nations (UN), Jews and Arabs in the Middle East agreed to put down their weapons and talk after several years of fierce fighting. Although the truce turned out to be only temporary, it was still a major accomplishment for the UN. And Bunche also proved his firm beliefs that no human relations problem is beyond resolution and that there are nonviolent ways to settle arguments. These beliefs shaped his course of action as a negotiator overseas and also at home, in the battle to gain civil rights for African Americans.

Early Life

Bunche was born in Detroit, Michigan, and spent his early childhood there. Due to his mother's poor health, however, he and his family moved to the milder climate of Albuquerque, New Mexico, when he was about ten. Three years

"LET US NOT FALL INTO THE FATAL ERROR OF ASCRIBING ALL OF OUR FAILURES TO RACIAL PREJUDICE. THE CRY OF DISCRIMINATION MUST NEVER BE USED AS AN ALIBI FOR LACK OF EFFORT, PREPARATION, AND ABILITY."

later, both of his parents died within just a few months of each other. Bunche and his sister then went to live with their maternal grandmother in Los Angeles, California. She was a very strong-willed woman who demanded the best for (and from) her grandchildren, especially her grandson.

Bunche had little trouble living up to her high standards. An outstanding student, he finished at the top of his high school class. He then went on to graduate with highest honors from the University of California at Los Angeles (UCLA) with a degree in international relations. He continued his studies at Harvard University, earning his master's degree in government in 1928. After spending four years in Washington, D.C., teaching at Howard University, Bunche returned to Harvard to work on his doctorate degree, which he received in 1934.

*Over the next few years, Bunche studied African **colonialism** and U.S. race relations at Northwestern University in Chicago, Illinois, the London School of Economics in London, England, and Capetown University in South Africa. He also served as co-director of the Institute of Race Relations at Swarthmore College in Pennsylvania and as a staff member of the Carnegie Corporation. It was while he was working for the Carnegie Corporation that he helped Swedish **sociologist** Gunnar Myrdal gather research for Myrdal's famous study of race relations in the United States,* An American Dilemma. *While researching the book in the deep South, Bunche and Myrdal were almost lynched twice.*

Enters Government Service

Bunche returned to teaching at Howard University in the late 1930s, remaining there until World War II began. He then went to work for the United States government. As an expert in colonial affairs, he held several important positions throughout the war years with the Office of Strategic Services (OSS, which later evolved into the Central Intelligence Agency, or CIA) and the State Department. He soon became one of the highest-ranking African Americans in the administration of President Franklin Roosevelt.

colonialism: the rule over a nation or territory by a foreign government.

sociologist: a person who studies human society, social institutions, and social relationships.

In addition to his regular duties, Bunche often served as the country's official representative at major international conferences. One of these was the 1945 meeting at which delegates from all over the world established a new organization known as the United Nations. Also in attendance at that historic meeting were **Mary McLeod Bethune** (see entry), another prominent African American advisor to President Roosevelt, and the head of Howard University, Mordecai Wyatt Johnson.

Joins the United Nations

In 1946, Bunche joined the United Nations as director of the trusteeship department. This job involved protecting the rights of people who lived in countries under colonial rule in parts of Asia, Africa, and the Middle East. In the years just after World War II, many of these countries began seeking independence from the European powers that had ruled them for decades or even centuries. Often, their attempts to win freedom led to war.

Things were especially tense in the Middle East, where there was pressure to create a new homeland for the thousands of European Jews who had been uprooted by World War II. UN officials recommended splitting the country of Palestine into separate Arab and Jewish states. Their decision aroused long-simmering hostilities between the two groups. Arabs in particular deeply resented having to give up any of their territory to people they regarded as outsiders.

Finally, in 1947, civil war broke out. The following year, after Israel was officially proclaimed the new Jewish state, other Arab countries joined in the fight. Meanwhile, UN negotiators led by Sweden's Count Folke Bernadotte worked behind the scenes to come up with a peaceful settlement.

Wins Nobel Prize

In September 1948, just four months after he began conducting peace talks, Count Bernadotte was assassinated. A new figure then emerged to lead the negotiators—Ralph Bunche. He was by then a skilled diplomat with a boundless sense of optimism (believing things will *work out well, no matter how bad they may seem at first). He continued the talks for some eleven months until both parties finally agreed to a truce in late 1949. It was a victory for the United Nations as well as for Bunche. His personal contribution was formally recognized in 1950 when he was awarded the Nobel Peace Prize—the first black ever to be so honored.*

*Bunche's work on behalf of world peace kept him extremely busy. As a result, he had less time that he would have liked to take part in the struggle for civil rights. Some of the more militant black activists of his era, including **Adam Clayton Powell, Jr.** (see entry), publicly criticized him for not taking a more active role in the movement. But whenever he was not involved in international affairs, Bunche did indeed take his place alongside other African Americans eager for change. He was, for example, a member of the board of directors of the National Association for the Advancement of Colored People (NAACP). He also participated in several major demonstrations led by **Martin Luther King, Jr.** (see entry), including the 1963 March on Washington and the 1965 Selma-to-Montgomery March. And as the civil rights struggle grew more militant during the mid-and late 1960s, Bunche added his voice to those who opposed any violent means of confrontation.*

In discussing the civil rights movement, Bunche often drew on his own experiences as a UN official to connect the African American quest for equal rights to the international scene. On numerous occasions, for instance, he warned that America could not possibly hope to inspire trust and admiration abroad if it continued to oppress minorities at home. This was his theme in a graduation speech he gave in Baltimore, Maryland, at Morgan State College (a historically black institution) on June 4, 1951. An excerpt from his remarks is reprinted here from the August 15, 1951, issue of Vital Speeches.

Throughout the nation during this month of June, thousands of young men and women ... will be

attending commencement exercises similar to these.... They will have very much on their minds what may lie ahead for them—whether there will be peace or war; what their chances may be for a promising career in their chosen fields of endeavor; how they may profitably and usefully employ the knowledge and training they have acquired.

But the Negro graduates at such exercises ... will have on their minds not only these thoughts, but some quite special ones, too, as they contemplate their future.... It is the great **irony** of our nation, a nation firmly dedicated to a democratic way of life, that a substantial proportion of its citizens must still overcome unjust and undemocratic racial handicaps, must surmount **arbitrary** obstacles of racial bigotry, in running the race of life. And this is so not because of any misdeeds, of any shortcomings, of any lack of industry, ability, or loyalty on the part of these citizens so handicapped. It is so only because they are Negroes, because of their color and race....

These graduates whom we honor today are to be doubly congratulated, for in coming this far they have had to meet not only the challenge of learning, they have had to learn over the handicaps of race—handicaps both economic and social.

And what has this meant and what will this mean for them? It means that all of them are fully acquainted with the Negro ghetto and the severe disadvantages it entails. They have had to endure the political and economic underprivilege which is synonymous with a segregated, separate, ghetto existence. Much of their life has unfolded thus far behind a cruel curtain of segregation and discrimination.

They know that their country was founded upon the sacred principles of the **inalienable** rights of man and the equality of all men before God. But they have been told that for Negroes this means only a qualified equality—separate equality, a separate existence from the rest of the community. They know too well the humiliation, the **degradation,** the psychological stresses and strains, the personality warping, which are the inevitable end-products of that separation. No one knows better than they that the doctrine of "separate but equal" is a monstrous fiction, an unabashed lie....

irony: contradiction, or a situation in which things are inconsistent with or opposite to each other.

arbitrary: determined randomly or by personal preference rather than logic or reason.

inalienable: unable to be withdrawn or given up.

degradation: a lowering in esteem, status, or conditions.

The practices and incidents of racial bigotry can only be intolerably offensive to every fair-minded and right-thinking American. They are costly to the nation in these dangerous times. They are costly because they raise serious doubts inter-nally and externally—about the true nature of the American democratic way of life.... Because they cannot fail to **induce** our friends abroad to doubt the genuineness of our democra-cy and to question our ability to treat nonwhite peoples any-where as equals. They are, therefore, tremendously damaging to our international prestige and to our leadership in the free world. And they hand to our enemies a most effective propa-ganda weapon in the worldwide **ideological** struggle—the struggle for the confidence of the peoples of the world, the **preponderance** of whom are nonwhite.

The heavy costs of racial prejudice in the American society are today being paid by every American citizen—white and black alike.... The security of our great nation, the way of life which is the source of our unparalleled national strength, are confronted with the most ominous challenge in our history. Never before have we so desperately needed our full strength and unity. But this is denied the nation only because some of our allegedly patriotic citizens insist upon continuing to indulge themselves in the social vice of racial prejudice....

This, surely, is not patriotism, nor is it good sense. It is sickness, or madness, or both.

Who, in his good senses, could doubt for an instant what it would mean to the strength, the unity, and the prestige of our nation if the cancerous growth of racial bigotry in the society were to be expelled?

This is all the Negro asks—that he be freed from the bondage of racial prejudice. Nothing more.... The Negro Amer-ican asks no special treatment from this society. He asks that nothing be given to him. He asks, or rather demands, only that he be permitted to enjoy what is rightfully his—his God-given, Constitution-guaranteed right to live and work and play in this society on the same basis as every other citizen....

If the society grants him that, and nothing short of that could ever be acceptable, the Negro problem is solved. This would in no way affect the right of any person in the society

induce: to bring about or cause.

ideological: having to do with the social and political beliefs of a particular group, country, or culture.

preponderance: majority.

to have as little or as much to do with any Negro, many Negroes, or all Negroes as he pleases....

I am not at all unmindful that the Negro citizen in the American society has made great progress, particularly in recent years. The barriers of segregation and discrimination are being beaten down, and in this effort the Negro has had much help from white Americans who believe in as well as **profess** democracy. I think it no exaggeration at all to say that no group of people in history has made as much progress in a comparable time as the Negro has made since his release from slavery. Moreover, I realize that this magnificent progress has been possible only because the Negro has been able to take increasing advantage of the opportunities for work, development, and struggle afforded by a society whose framework is free and democratic.

But the fact remains, nevertheless, that these graduates before us today, despite the fine training they have received here, will go out into the world and encounter unique obstacles in shaping their careers only because they are Negroes.... They will not enjoy their full rights as American citizens, and until Negro graduates and all other Negroes can do so the American society will be guilty of a terrible injustice....

It is important that these Negro graduates bear in mind that though the Negro has made and is making great progress, very much remains to be done. The road immediately ahead will never be easy. The rate of progress will depend in large degree upon the preparation and ability, the determination, and the courage of these young Negroes. They must never relax in the struggle for full citizenship for the Negro, for the complete integration of American Negroes in the life of the nation....

In this regard there are certain truths which the Negro citizen must learn well and bear constantly in mind.

In a democratic society—and we are greatly privileged to live in one, the world being as it is these days—the Negro citizen like all other citizens must willingly and self-sacrificingly assume heavy responsibilities and obligations in return for the rights and freedoms which he may enjoy. Democracy gives no free rides. The Negro cannot be a good citizen if he concentrates exclusively on the problems of his group. All of

profess: openly declare belief in and loyalty to certain principles.

the problems of his community and nation are his problems and the Negro must devote his intelligent interest and effort to them. Integration in the society is a two-way proposition. The more integrated the Negro becomes the heavier will his civic responsibilities become....

Because of discrimination, the Negro has much to complain of, but let us not fall into the fatal error of **ascribing** all of our failures to racial prejudice. The cry of discrimination must never be used as an **alibi** for lack of effort, preparation, and ability. We can never end discrimination by hiding behind it, or as I fear some Negroes do, by acquiring a **vested interest** in it.

It is well also to bear always in mind in this hard world that fate helps only those who help themselves. We are much stronger now than we were and we can utilize our own resources of ability and wealth to much better advantage than in earlier years. I wonder if we really do as much for ourselves as we might, if we are as united and resolved as we should be.... In my view, no Negro, however high he may have risen, is worth very much if he forgets his people and remains **aloof** from the unrelenting struggle for full Negro emancipation.

Let us also be aware of the unfortunate **inclination** of the Negro himself to tighten the bonds of the ghetto by ghetto thinking. Life in the ghetto tempts the Negro to make the Negro problem the pivotal point of his thinking, as though everything in the world revolves about this problem. This is racial **provincialism** of the worst kind, and can only retard the progress of the group. It develops a narrowness of mind and a racial **egocentrism,** which is bad for both the Negro and the society in which he lives....

I am reasonably optimistic about the future of race relations in America. The conscience of the nation quickens. An ever-increasing number of citizens, South as well as North, realize that our bad race relations are immensely damaging to the nation, and they are determined to do something about it. The forces of true democracy are strongly at work in our society and the force of democracy on the march is irresistible....

You graduates have no reason to be discouraged or pessimistic about the future before you. You can surmount the obstacles in your path if you are determined, courageous, and

ascribing: blaming, attributing.

alibi: an excuse intended to escape personal blame.

vested interest: a special and often secret concern for maintaining something the way it is, especially for selfish reasons.

aloof: distant, uninvolved.

inclination: natural disposition or character, or personal preference.

provincialism: the tendency to focus one's outlook on a very small area and ignore the world at large.

egocentrism: self-centeredness, or regarding oneself and one's needs and activities as more important than anyone or anything else.

Ralph Bunche

hard-working. Never be faint-hearted. Be **resolute,** but never bitter. Bitterness will serve only to warp your personality. Permit no one to **dissuade** you from pursuing the goals you set for yourselves. In this country, difficult as it may be for you compared with others of fairer skin, no achievement is beyond you. Do not fear to pioneer, to venture down new paths of endeavor. Demand and make good use of your rights, but never fail to **discharge** faithfully the obligations and responsibilities of good citizenship. Be good Americans.

You are to be congratulated on having journeyed this far. You will, I am sure, be valuable assets to your group, your community, and your nation. You will have much to do with the shaping of the nation's future.

I salute you and I wish you well.

99

Bunche never lost hope that there were peaceful solutions to the many conflicts raging at home and overseas. After receiving the Nobel Prize, he devoted the rest of his career to developing peacekeeping strategies while negotiating disputes in places like the Congo (now known as Zaire), Cyprus, the Suez Canal, India, and Pakistan. In 1968, he was named under-secretary general of the United Nations, the highest rank ever held by an American. He died in December 1971, about six months after a series of illnesses had forced him to retire from his job.

Sources

Books

Baird, A. Craig, editor, *Representative American Speeches: 1949–1950,* Wilson, 1950.

Bunche, Ralph, *A World View of Race,* Association in Negro Folk Education, 1936, reprinted, Kennikat, 1968.

Foner, Philip S., editor, *The Voice of Black America: Major Speeches by Negroes in the United States, 1797-1971,* Simon & Schuster, 1972.

Haberman, Frederick W., editor, *Nobel Lectures: Peace, 1926–1950,* Volume 2, Elsevier, 1972.

resolute: determined, bold.

dissuade: advise against or turn one from.

discharge: perform, fulfill.

Hale, Frank W., Jr., editor, *The Cry for Freedom: An Anthology of the Best That Has Been Said and Written on Civil Rights since 1954,* A. S. Barnes & Co., 1969.

Haskins, Jim, *Ralph Bunche: A Most Reluctant Hero,* Hawthorn, 1974.

Kugelmass, J. Alvin, *Ralph J. Bunche: Fighter for Peace,* Messner, 1962.

Mann, Peggy, *Ralph Bunche: UN Peacemaker,* Coward, McCann & Geoghegan, 1975.

Reid, Loren, editor, *American Public Address: Studies in Honor of Albert Craig Baird* (contains chapter entitled "Ralph Bunche: Negro Spokesman"), University of Missouri Press, 1961.

Urquhart, Brian, *Ralph Bunche: An American Life,* Norton, 1993.

Williams, Jamye Coleman, and McDonald Williams, editors, *The Negro Speaks: The Rhetoric of Contemporary Black Leaders,* Noble & Noble, 1970.

Periodicals

Nation, "Ralph Bunche," December 27, 1971.

Newsweek, "Never Did He Despair," October 11, 1971, pp. 44-49; "Ralph Bunche, 1904-1971," December 20, 1971, p. 33.

New York Times, December 10, 1971.

Time, "Man Without Color," December 20, 1971, pp. 34-39.

Vital Speeches, "The Barriers of Race Can Be Surmounted," July 1, 1949; "Freedom Is Blessing, Not a License," August 15, 1951; "The Road to Peace," August 15, 1954.

Yale Review, "Remembering Ralph Bunche," spring, 1987, pp. 448-451.

Stokely Carmichael (Kwame Touré)

1941–

Political and social activist

During the mid- and late 1960s, Stokely Carmichael stood at the forefront of the Black Power movement. (In fact, he is even given credit for coining the phrase "Black Power.") A militant offshoot of the mainstream civil rights struggle, the Black Power movement brought back to life the ideas of earlier black nationalists such as **Marcus Garvey** *(see entry). (A black nationalist is a person who believes that African Americans should separate from whites to form their own self-governing communities and businesses.) Carmichael was known as the movement's most effective and popular speaker as well as one of its most creative thinkers.*

Early Life

Carmichael was a native of the Caribbean island nation of Trinidad. He moved to New York City with his family when he was eleven and grew up in the ghetto. Later, while attending Howard University, he participated in the student sit-ins

"I MAINTAIN THAT EVERY CIVIL RIGHTS BILL IN THIS COUNTRY WAS PASSED FOR WHITE PEOPLE, NOT FOR BLACK PEOPLE."

sponsored by the Congress of Racial Equality (CORE). (A sit-in is an act of organized protest in which protestors occupy a building or organization by sitting in its seats or on its floors.)

*After graduating from college in 1964, Carmichael joined the Student Nonviolent Coordinating Committee (SNCC), a protest organization that had always emphasized nonviolent methods such as sit-ins. Just two years later, he became head of SNCC and began moving quickly to change its philosophy. Carmichael rejected the strategy of nonviolent resistance, for example. Instead, he warned that if black demonstrators were attacked by whites, the blacks would respond with attacks of their own. He also put an end to the practice of allowing white **liberals** to hold key roles in the organization.*

Develops Major Themes of the Black Power Movement

*As a promoter of Black Power, Carmichael urged African Americans to take pride in their heritage and achievements. (This idea was symbolized by the popular expression "black is beautiful.") He also told them to demand complete political, social, economic, and cultural independence from white institutions. He condemned **integration** as something that denied the value of blackness by making it seem like the only path to success in life was through ways that whites had created and approved. Cleaver also felt that integration was harmful to the future of African Americans because it tended to pull the most talented black people out of their communities to serve white interests.*

*The idea of Black Power left many people—white as well as black—frightened and suspicious. They thought it was another way of describing black racial hatred and violence. This image was enhanced by media coverage of the movement, which often relied on **sensationalism** and exaggeration to make Black Power activists appear dangerous.*

In October 1966, Carmichael spoke at the Berkeley Black Power Conference in California. In his address to a largely white student audience, he discussed racism and how advocates of black power planned to put an end to it. An excerpt from the speech is taken from Carmichael's own

liberals: people who are broad-minded and not inclined to follow tradition or reject change.

integration: to bring different groups into mainsteam society as equals.

sensationalism: using or treating subject matter in a way that arouses intense excitement, curiosity, or emotion.

Stokely Carmichael (Kwame Touré)

book, Stokely Speaks: Black Power Back to Pan-African-ism, *Random House, 1971.*

66

...The [French existentialist] philosophers [Albert] Camus and [Jean-Paul] Sartre raise the question of whether or not a man can condemn himself. [Existentialism is a philosophy that maintains each individual has freedom of choice in deciding how to act or what to become in life, but that he or she must also take responsibility for the outcome, because there is no certain knowledge of right and wrong in the world.] The black existentialist philosopher who is **pragmatic,** Frantz Fanon, answered the question. He said that man could not.... We in SNCC tend to agree with Fanon—a man cannot condemn himself. If he did, he would then have to inflict punishment upon himself.

An example is the Nazis [during World War II]. Any of the Nazi prisoners who, after he was caught and **incarcerated,** admitted that ... he killed all the many people he killed, had to commit suicide. The only ones able to stay alive were the ones who never admitted that they committed a crime against people—that is, the ones who **rationalized** that Jews were not human beings and deserved to be killed, or that they were only following orders.

There's another, more recent example provided by the officials and the population—the white population—of Neshoba County, Mississippi.... They could not condemn Sheriff [Lawrence] Rainey, his deputies, and the other fourteen men who killed three human beings. [Carmichael is referring here to the murders of civil rights workers James Chaney, Andrew Goodman, and Michael Schwerner, whose bodies were discovered buried in a shallow grave outside Philadelphia, Mississippi, in August 1964. The FBI accused nearly two dozen white segregationists—including several law enforcement officers—of the crime.] They could not because they elected Mr. Rainey to do precisely what he did; and condemning him would be condemning themselves.

In a much larger view, SNCC says that white America cannot condemn herself for her criminal acts against black

pragmatic: practical, realistic.

incarcerated: imprisoned.

rationalized: attributed one's actions to reasonable motives without acknowledging the other unconscious or emotional motivations behind one's conduct.

America. So black people have done it.... The institutions that function in this country are clearly racist; they're built upon racism. The questions to be dealt with then are: How can black people inside this country move? How can white people who say they're not part of those institutions begin to move? And how then do we begin to clear away the obstacles that we have in this society, to make us live like human beings?...

In the past six years or so, this country has been feeding us a "thalidomide drug of integration," and some Negroes have been walking down a dream street talking about sitting next to white people. That does not begin to solve the problem. We didn't go to Mississippi to sit next to Ross Barnett [former governor of Mississippi], we did not go to sit next to Jim Clark [sheriff of Selma, Alabama], we went to get them out of our way. People ought to understand that; we were never fighting for the right to integrate, we were fighting against **white supremacy.** In order to understand white supremacy we must dismiss the **fallacious** notion that white people can give anybody his freedom. A man is born free. You may enslave a man after he is born free, and that is in fact what this country does....

I maintain that every civil rights bill in this country was passed for white people, not for black people. For example, I am black. I know that. I also know that while I am black I am a human being. Therefore I have the right to go into any public place. White people didn't know that. Every time I tried to go into a public place they stopped me. So some boys had to write a bill to tell that white man, "He's a human being; don't stop him." That bill was for the white man, not for me.

I knew I could vote all the time and that it wasn't a privilege but my right. Every time I tried I was shot, killed or jailed, beaten or economically deprived. So somebody had to write a bill to tell white people, "When a black man comes to vote, don't bother him." That bill was for white people.

I know I can live anyplace I want to live. It is white people across this country who are incapable of allowing me to live where I want. You need a civil rights bill, not me. The failure of the civil rights bill isn't because of Black Power or because

white supremacy: the idea that whites are a superior group of people entitled to full power and authority.

fallacious: false.

Stokely Carmichael (Kwame Touré)

of the Student Nonviolent Coordinating Committee or because of the rebellions that are occurring in the major cities. That failure is due to the whites' incapacity to deal with their own problems inside their own communities.

And so in a sense we must ask, How is it that black people move? And what do we do? But the question in a much greater sense is, How can white people who are the majority, and who are responsible for making democracy work, make it work? They have failed miserably on this point.... We not only condemn the country for what it has done internally, but we must condemn it for what it does externally. We see this country trying to rule the world, and someone must stand up and start **articulating** that this country is not God, and that it cannot rule the world.

The white supremacist attitude, which you have either consciously or subconsciously, is running rampant through society today. For example, missionaries were sent to Africa with the attitude that blacks were automatically inferior.... When the missionaries came to civilize us because we were uncivilized..., they charged a price. The missionaries came with the Bible, and we had the land; when they left, they had the land, and we still have the Bible.

That's been the rationalization for Western civilization as it moves across the world—stealing, plundering and raping everybody in its path. Their one rationalization is that the rest of the world is uncivilized and they are in fact civilized.... Now we have "modern-day missionaries," and they come into our ghettos—they Head Start, Upward Lift, Bootstrap, and Upward Bound us into white society. They don't want to face the real problem. A man is poor for one reason and one reason only—he does not have money. If you want to get rid of poverty, you give people money. And you ought not to tell me about people who don't work, and that you can't give people money if they don't work, because if that were true,

Carmichael speaking, 1966: "We're not going to wait for white people to sanction Black Power."

articulating: saying clearly and effectively.

you'd have to start stopping Rockefeller, Kennedy, [President] Lyndon Baines Johnson, Lady Bird Johnson, the whole of Standard Oil, the Gulf Corporation, all of them, including probably a large number of the board of trustees of this university. The question, then, is not whether or not one can work; it's who has power to make his or her acts **legitimate?** That is all. In this country that power is invested in the hands of white people, and it makes their acts legitimate.

We are now engaged in a psychological struggle in this country about whether or not black people have the right to use the words they want to use without white people giving their **sanction....** We are not going to wait for white people to sanction Black Power. We're tired of waiting; every time black people try to move in this country, they're forced to defend their position beforehand. It's time that white people do that. They ought to start defending themselves as to why they have **oppressed** and **exploited** us. A man was picked as a slave for one reason—the color of his skin. Black was automatically inferior, inhuman, and therefore fit for slavery.... We are oppressed as a group because we are black, not because we are lazy or **apathetic,** not because we're stupid or we stink, not because we eat watermelon or have good rhythm....

In order to escape that oppression we must **wield** the group power we have, not the individual power that this country sets as the **criterion** under which a man may come into it. That's what is called integration. "You do what I tell you to do and we'll let you sit at the table with us." Well, if you believe in integration, you can come live in Watts [a black ghetto in Los Angeles, California], send your children to the ghetto schools....

The political parties of this country do not meet the needs of the people on a day-to-day basis. How can we build new political institutions that will become the political expressions of people? How can you build political institutions that will begin to meet the needs of Oakland, California? The need of Oakland, California, is not a thousand policemen with submachine guns.... How can we build institutions that will allow those people to function on a day-to-day basis, so that they can get decent jobs and have decent houses, and they can begin to participate in the policy and make the

legitimate: accepted, recognized.

sanction: approval.

oppressed: crushed or persecuted through the abuse of power or authority.

exploited: unfairly used another person for one's own profit.

apathetic: showing a lack of emotion or concern.

wield: use as a tool or an instrument of authority.

criterion: rule, standard.

Stokely Carmichael (Kwame Touré)

decisions that affect their lives? That's what they need, not **Gestapo troops,** because this is not 1942, and if you play like Nazis, we're not going to play Jew this time around. Get hip to that....

White people make sure that we live in the ghettos of this country. White institutions do that. They must change. In order for America to really live on a basic principle of human relationships, a new society must be born. Racism must die. The economic exploitation by this country of nonwhite people around the world must also die.

There are several programs in the South where whites are trying to organize poor whites so they can begin to move around the question of economic exploitation and political **disfranchisement.** We've all heard the theory several times. But few people are willing to go into it. The question is, Can the white activist stop trying to be a Pepsi generation who comes alive in the black community, and be a man who's willing to move into the white community and start organizing where the organization is needed?...

Most white activists run into the black community as an excuse. We cannot have white people working in the black community—on psychological grounds. The fact is that all black people question whether or not they are equal to whites, since every time they start to do something, white people are around showing them how to do it. If we are going to eliminate that for the generation that comes after us, then black people must be in positions of power, doing and articulating for themselves. That's not reverse racism; it is moving onto healthy ground.... And this country can't understand that. What we have in SNCC is antiracist racism.... We are against racists....

We have found all the myths of the country to be nothing but downright lies. We were told that if we worked hard we would succeed, and if that were true we would own this country lock, stock, and barrel. We have picked the cotton for nothing; we are the maids in the kitchens of liberal white people; we are the janitors, the porters, the elevator men; we sweep up your college floors. We are the hardest workers and the lowest paid. It is nonsensical for people to talk about human relationships until they are willing to build new insti-

Gestapo troops: secret police in Nazi Germany who often used terrorism and deception to frighten and threaten suspects.

disfranchisement: denial of the right to vote.

tutions. Black people are economically insecure. White liberals are economically secure. Can you begin to build an economic **coalition?** Are the liberals willing to share their salaries with the economically insecure black people they so much love? Then if you're not, are you willing to start building new institutions that will provide economic security for black people? That's the question we want to deal with!

American students are perhaps the most politically **unsophisticated** students in the world. Across every country of the world, while we were growing up, students were leading the major revolutions of their countries.... They have been politically aware of their existence.... But we have been unable to grasp it because we've always moved in the field of morality and love while people have been politically jiving with our lives. You can't move morally against men like [California Governor Pat] Brown and [Ronald] Reagan [who was then running for governor of California]. You can't move morally against Lyndon Baines Johnson because he is an immoral man.... So you've got to move politically.... We have to raise questions about whether we need new types of political institutions in this country, and we in SNCC maintain that we need them now....

We must question the values of this society, and I maintain that black people are the best people to do that since we have been excluded from that society. We ought to think whether or not we want to become a part of that society....

White society has caused the failure of nonviolence. I was always surprised at Quakers who came to Alabama and counseled me to be nonviolent, but didn't have the guts to tell [Sheriff] James Clark to be nonviolent.... Can you name one black man today who has killed anybody white and is still alive? Even after a rebellion, when some black brothers throw bricks and bottles, ten thousand of them have to pay the price....

The youth of this country must begin to raise those questions. We are going to have to change the foreign policy of this country.... We have to hook up with black people around the world; and that hookup must not only be psychological, but real....

coalition: an alliance of different people or groups who come together to take action.

unsophisticated: lacking knowledge and experience.

Stokely Carmichael (Kwame Touré)

How do we stop those institutions that are so willing to fight against "Communist aggression" but close their eyes against racist oppression? We're not talking about a policy of aid or sending Peace Corps people in to teach people how to read and write and build houses while we steal their raw materials from them. Because that's all this country does. What underdeveloped countries need is information about how to become industrialized, so they can keep their raw materials where they have them, produce goods, sell them to this country for the price it's supposed to pay. Instead, America keeps selling goods back to them for a profit and keeps sending our modern-day missionaries there....

This country assumes that if someone is poor, they are poor because of their own individual blight, or because they weren't

Carmichael at a University of California rally

born on the right side of town, or they had too many children, or went in the army too early, or because their father was a drunk, or they didn't care about school—they made a mistake. That's a lot of nonsense. Poverty is well **calculated** in this country, and the reason why the poverty program won't work is because the calculators of poverty are administering it....

This country knows what power is. It knows what Black Power is because it deprived black people of it for over four hundred years. White people associate Black Power with violence because of their own inability to deal with blackness. If we had said "Negro power" nobody would get scared. Everybody would support it. If we said power for colored people, everybody'd be for that, but it is the word "black" that bothers people in this country, and that's their problem, not mine. That's the lie that says anything black is bad....

I'm never going to be put in that bag; I'm all black and I'm all good. Anything all black is not necessarily bad. Anything all black is only bad when you use force to keep whites out. Now that's what white people have done in this country, and they're projecting their same fears and guilt on us, and we won't have it. Let them handle their own affairs and their own guilt. Let them find their own psychologists. We refuse to be the therapy for white society any longer. We have gone stark, raving mad trying to do it....

If we were to be real and honest, we would have to admit that most people in this country see things black and white. We live in a country that's geared that way. White people would have to admit that they are afraid to go into a black ghetto at night.... Since white people are afraid of that, they get a man to do it for them—a policeman. Figure his mentality. The first time a black man jumps, that white man's going to shoot him. Police brutality is going to exist on that level. The only time I hear people talk about nonviolence is when black people move to defend themselves against white people.... You show me a black man who advocates aggressive violence who would be able to live in this country....

We must wage a psychological battle on the right for black people to define themselves as they see fit, and organize themselves as they see fit. We don't know whether the white community will allow for that organizing, because once they

calculated: carefully and deliberately planned.

Stokely Carmichael (Kwame Touré)

do they must also allow for the organizing inside their own community. It doesn't make a difference, though—we're going to organize our way. The question is how we're going to **facilitate** those matters, whether it's going to be done with a thousand policemen with submachine guns, or whether it's going to be done in a context where it's allowed by white people.... We must urge you to fight now to be the leaders of today, not tomorrow. This country is a nation of thieves. It stands on the brink of becoming a nation of murderers. We must stop it. We must stop it. We must stop it.

We are on the move for our liberation. We're tired of trying to prove things to white people. We are tired of trying to explain to white people that we're not going to hurt them. We are concerned with getting the things we want, the things we have to have to be able to function. The question is, Will white people overcome their racism and allow for that to happen in this country? If not, we have no choice but to say very clearly, "Move on over, or we're going to move on over you."

" "

*By 1968, Carmichael had left SNCC to join the far more militant Black Panthers (see entry on **Eldridge Cleaver** for more information). He did not remain a Black Panther for long, however. Even before leaving SNCC, he had given up on the idea that black and white radicals might be able to work together. Thus, when the Black Panthers began taking steps to link up with white radicals, he let it be known that he was against forming any such coalition.*

Carmichael's objections fell on deaf ears, so in 1969 he resigned from the Black Panthers and moved to Africa. There, under the name Kwame Touré (also spelled Turé), he has worked for the Pan-African movement—a movement working for closer ties and political unity among all people of African descent. Its goal is to broaden the struggle against racial oppression to include blacks from all over the world. And Touré still believes that one day the poor will band together and overthrow the current economic and political system in favor of a socialist system (an economic

facilitate: assist, make easier.

and political system that involves government management of the production and distribution of goods and services).

In early 1996, Touré was forced to cut back on his political and social activism while he battled cancer. Diagnosed while on one of his regular visits to the United States, he remained in New York City for several weeks and then traveled to Cuba for treatment of the disease.

Sources

Books

Bracey, John H., Jr., August Meier, and Elliott Rudwick, editors, *Black Nationalism in America,* Bobbs-Merrill, 1970.

Carmichael, Stokely, *Stokely Speaks: Black Power Back to Pan-Africanism,* Random House, 1971.

Carmichael, Stokely, and Charles Hamilton, *Black Power: The Politics of Liberation in America,* Random House, 1967.

Carson, Clayborne, and others, editors, *The Eyes on the Prize Civil Rights Reader,* Penguin, 1991.

Foner, Philip S., editor, *The Voice of Black America: Major Speeches by Negroes in the United States, 1797–1971,* Simon & Schuster, 1972.

Holland, DeWitte, editor, *America in Controversy: History of American Public Address,* William C. Brown Company, 1973.

Johnson, Jacqueline, *Stokely Carmichael: The Story of Black Power,* Silver Burdett, 1990.

Lomas, Charles W., *The Agitator in American Society,* Prentice-Hall, 1968.

Scott, Robert L., and Wayne Brockriede, *The Rhetoric of Black Power,* Harper & Row, 1969.

Smith, Arthur L., and Stephen Robb, editors, *The Voice of Black Rhetoric: Selections,* Allyn & Bacon, 1971.

Williams, Jamye Coleman, and McDonald Williams, editors, *The Negro Speaks: The Rhetoric of Contemporary Black Leaders,* Noble and Noble, 1970.

Periodicals

Ebony, "Stokely Carmichael: Architect of Black Power," September 1966.

Massachusetts Review, "Toward Black Liberation," September 1966, pp. 639–651

New York Review of Books, September 22, 1966, pp. 5–8.

People, "A Panther in Winter," April 22, 1996, pp. 63-64.

Saturday Review, "The Real Stokely Carmichael," July 9, 1966.

Other

"Black Americans: Stokely Carmichael" (audiocassette of interview on *Face the Nation* television program, June 19, 1966), Holt Information Systems, c. 1973.

"Stokely Carmichael" (audiocassette of interview, February 1975), Pacifica Tape Library, 1975.

Ben Carson

1941–
Neurosurgeon

"IN HIGH SCHOOL, I RAN INTO PERHAPS THE WORST THING A YOUNG PERSON CAN RUN INTO—IT'S CALLED *peers*. NEGATIVE *peers*. P-E-E-R-S. THAT STANDS FOR 'PEOPLE WHO ENCOURAGE ERRORS, RUDENESS, AND STUPIDITY.'"

In September 1987, a young black doctor in Baltimore made headlines all over the world when he successfully separated Siamese twins Patrick and Benjamin Binder. The little boys' bodies had been joined together in a tangled mass of blood vessels at the back of each of their heads. In similar cases, this very complicated operation had always ended in death or severe brain damage for at least one of the children involved. But Dr. Ben Carson—an easy-going, soft-spoken man known as "Gentle Ben" to his coworkers and patients—was eager to defy the odds. In fact, the challenge that greeted him that day was just the latest in a number of challenges he has had to face on the road to becoming one of the world's best pediatric **neurosurgeons** (doctors who specialize in operating on the nerves, the brain, and the spinal cord).

Early Life

Carson was born and raised in Detroit, Michigan,

except for a two-year period when he lived with relatives in Boston, Massachusetts. He grew up in a single-parent household after his parents divorced when he was eight years old. His mother, Sonya Carson, who struggled hard to provide for herself and her two young sons, worried constantly that they would follow the self-destructive path of so many of the other boys in the neighborhood. Although both youngsters were very bright, they did poorly in school. Ben in particular had a quick temper that often got him into serious trouble.

Thanks to Sonya Carson's persistence, however, the two boys slowly began to turn their lives around. Her plan of action centered around turning off the television set in the evening and reading instead. Ben was fascinated by what he discovered in the pages of the books he checked out of the library. He soon developed a passion for science and decided he wanted to become a doctor. By the time he reached seventh grade, he had improved his schoolwork so much that he was at the top of his class.

Around the same time, Ben learned another life-changing lesson—how important it was to control his temper. One day, he was with some friends listening to the radio when one of them switched the station and then refused to switch back. Furious, Ben attacked the other boy with a knife, which hit a metal belt buckle and broke. Frightened and upset, both boys immediately ran home. Ben spent the next few hours agonizing over how close he had come to injuring—or even killing—his friend. He pledged then and there never to give in to his anger again.

With his life at last on track, Ben continued to excel in school. He graduated third in his high school class and then went on to Yale University on a scholarship. From there, he headed to medical school at the University of Michigan. After earning his degree, he was accepted into the prestigious residency program at Baltimore's Johns Hopkins Hospital, where he decided to specialize in neurosurgery. Carson then spent a year working as chief resident at a hospital in Australia. The shortage of neurosurgeons in Australia left him with a very heavy workload. But it also gave him the chance to gain much more experience than

Ben Carson with model of human brain

he ever would have obtained had he stayed in the United States.

Head of Pediatric Neurosurgery at Johns Hopkins Hospital

Soon after his return to Baltimore in 1984, Carson was named head of the department of pediatric neurosurgery at

Johns Hopkins Hospital. He was only thirty-three years old at the time—the youngest doctor in the country to hold such a position. Since then, he has earned a reputation as an extremely compassionate and skillful surgeon willing to take on the toughest cases, mostly those involving children with severe neurological problems.

*Carson is an enthusiastic fan of using modern technology to make the impossible possible. He was, for example, the first doctor to perform brain surgery on a fetus inside the womb. He has also achieved tremendous success performing a very risky operation known as a hemispherectomy. In a hemispherectomy, the surgeon removes half of the patient's brain to stop the crippling seizures caused by a rare and **chronic** form of encephalitis, or inflammation of the brain. Until Carson came along, most doctors wouldn't even try to do the surgery because so few patients survived.*

The case of the Binder Siamese twins presented Carson with a different set of problems. The way they were joined at the back of each of their heads seemed to doom them to heavy blood loss (and probably death) during surgery. Carson spent several months creating an entirely new approach that borrowed from the techniques surgeons use in heart operations. He decided he would stop the babies' hearts, drain all of their blood, and then work quickly to separate them before restoring their circulation.

The creative new method worked, and Carson soon found himself showered with media attention by those who were interested in knowing exactly how he had done it. Many of these same people also wanted to learn more about the personal background of this apparent miracle-worker. Before long, news of his inspiring journey to the top of his profession had made him a celebrity.

Now in constant demand as a speaker, Carson willingly shares the story of his life and his formula for success with a variety of audiences across the country. For example, on June 27, 1994, in Dallas, Texas, he spoke at the annual meeting of the Million Dollar Round Table (MDRT), a group of highly successful life insurance agents. Portions of the

chronic: happening frequently or over a long period of time.

speech he delivered at the convention have been transcribed from an audiotape available through the MDRT.

66

The week before last, I was in South Africa. I had been asked to come over there to help try to separate Siamese twins that were joined at the head. And this, of course, was a very complex endeavor. Well, it turned out that the surgical separation was extremely difficult technically but went very well. However, the twins did not survive, because they were something that had never been described before—they were ... living off each other. One had the cardiac [heart] function for both, and one had the renal [kidney] function for both. So even though we were able to separate them, they were unable to survive apart from each other, and they were in the process of dying together, because the one who had the cardiac function was rapidly deteriorating because he couldn't work hard enough for both of them.

Nevertheless, we learned some very important things from that—things that will be very useful to the medical community as life goes on. And it brings up one of the themes in my life, one of the things I tell young people all the time—that there is no such thing as failure as long as you learn from it. You have to be able to take something away from every incident. That's why we have these complex brains which allow us to process information and to move ahead....

I really got interested in medicine because I would listen to the mission stories in church, and they frequently featured missionary doctors. There were stories about how these people, at great personal sacrifice, would go out into the world and bring not only physical, but mental and spiritual healing to people. And I said, "What a *wonderful* thing! How could *anybody* do anything more *magnificent* than that?" I harbored that dream of being a missionary doctor from the age of eight until I was thirteen, when, having grown up in dire poverty, I decided I'd rather be rich.

So at that point, I wanted to be a psychiatrist. Now, I didn't *know* any psychiatrists, but at least on television they lived in these big, fancy houses with gates and fountains, and they drove Jaguars, and they had these big plush offices, and all they had to do was talk to crazy people all day! It seemed like I was doing that anyway, so I said, this will be a fantastic way to get very rich! I started reading *Psychology Today,* majored in psychology, did advanced psych when I went to medical school. That's when I started meeting a bunch of psychiatrists. And I don't think I need say more about *that*.

Now, actually, I should say some of my best friends are psychiatrists. There's nothing wrong with psychiatrists, it's just that I discovered that my concept of psychiatry had been **gleaned** from television. A lot of our young people glean their concepts of the world from television, and these are some of the most inaccurate portrayals imaginable to man. We have to be very careful about making sure that our young people really understand the world that they're going out into.

I think back—at age eight, my parents got divorced. My mother had only a third-grade education and the responsibility of trying to raise two young sons in inner-city Detroit with no money and very little hope. But she had some wisdom, and she decided we would move to Boston to live with her older sister and brother-in-law in one of the tenements in Boston. It was a typical tenement with large, multi-family dwellings, broken glass on the streets, boarded-up windows and doors, and gangs and sirens and murders....

While we were out there enjoying that environment, my mother was out working two—frequently three—jobs at a time trying to stay off of welfare. She didn't want to be on welfare, she wanted to be in control of her own life. She was a person who would never adopt what I call the "victim's mentality." I think that's one of the essential things that she was able to pass along to my brother and myself, and I frequently thank her for that. After working for a couple of years, she was, in fact, able to gain some degree of independence. We were able to move back to Detroit....

I was a fifth-grader. And I'll tell you, my idea of a good time was to goof off all day in school. My favorite subject was recess, and then to go home and play outside—baseball, football, basketball, kickball, throwing rocks at cars—whatever.

gleaned: obtained.

And then when it was too dark, to go inside and watch TV till bedtime. As a result of that philosophy, I had no competition for last spot in my class. No one ever had to worry about getting the worst mark on anything as long as I was around. I was the safety net, you might say. I believed that I was stupid, and everybody else did....

My mother was very discouraged when she saw my fifth-grade report card at midterm and I was failing almost every subject. She didn't know what to do. My brother was also doing poorly. She prayed and she asked God to give her wisdom. What could she do to get her young sons to understand the importance of developing their minds intellectually so that they could have control of their own lives? And you know something? God gave her the wisdom, at least in her opinion. My brother and I didn't think it was all that wise, because it was to turn off the TV set, let us watch only two or three TV programs during the week, and with all that spare time, we had to read two books apiece from the Detroit Public Library *and* submit to her written book reports which she couldn't read—but we didn't know that. So, in fact, she had pulled a fast one on us, but we didn't know it.

I was kind of a rebellious fellow, so I said, well, I'm gonna get books that have a lot of pictures in them, and I'll just report on the pictures. But those pictures were so interesting, pretty soon I wanted to read the legend beneath the picture, and the page next to the picture. And the pictures became less important, and the reading became much *more* important.

I started reading about all kinds of things, and all kinds of careers where people used their intellect—astronomers, astronauts, research chemists, surgeons—and I started saying, this is something that maybe *I* can do. I really got interested in animals.... Then I started reading about plants. But the thing that really grabbed my attention was rocks, because we lived near the railroad tracks. And what is there along the railroad tracks? Rocks! So I would collect little boxes of rocks, bring them home, get my geology books from the library, and compare the rocks with the pictures. Pretty soon I could identify virtually any rock, tell you where it came from, how it was formed. Still in the fifth grade, still the dummy in the class—nobody knew about this project.

And one day the fifth-grade science teacher walked in, held up a big black shiny rock, [and] says, "Can *anybody* tell me what this is?" Well, as the dummy of the class, I *never* raised my hand. So I waited for one of the *smart* kids to raise their hand. And none of them did! So I waited for one of the *dumb* kids to raise their hand. And none of *them* did! I said, this is it, it's my big chance, and up went my hand.

And *everybody* turned around, they looked, they were poking each other; this was something they'd never seen before—me with my hand up! The teacher called on me, and I said, "Mr. Jake, that's obsidian." There was silence in the room. Because it *sounded* good, and nobody knew whether it was right or wrong, and they didn't know whether they should be laughing, or whether they should be impressed. Finally, Mr. Jake said, "That's right! It *is* obsidian!" And I said, "You know, obsidian is formed after a volcanic eruption. The lava flows down, it hits the water, there's a super-cooling process, and the elements coalesce, and the air is forced out, and the surface glazes...." Everybody was *staring* at me! Their mouths were hanging open. They couldn't believe all this geological information spewing forth from the mouth of the dummy.

But *I* was perhaps the most amazed person because it dawned on me at that moment that I wasn't dumb after all. I said, Carson, the reason you knew those answers is because you were reading those books. I said, now suppose you read books about all your other subjects—science and math and history and geography and social studies—I said, couldn't you then know more than *all* these students who love to tease you? And I must say the idea appealed to me to the extent that no book was safe in my grasp. I read everything in sight. And within the space of a year-and-a-half, I went from no competition for last spot to no competition for first spot in my class....

Things *really* started rolling for me at that point. It's very important to understand that when I was in the fifth grade, and I took a test, I expected to get the lowest mark on it, and I generally did. When I was in the *seventh* grade, and I took a test, I expected to get the *highest* mark, and I generally did. I did *not* have a brain transplant in between. It tells you something about the human mind, the human capacity, and how to use it appropriately....

You would've thought that maybe after I learned all these things I would be OK. But you see, then I went to high school. I was a straight-A student until I got to the tenth grade, and then I ran into perhaps the worst thing a young person can run into—it's called *peers*. Negative *peers*. P-e-e-r-s. That stands for "people who encourage errors, rudeness, and stupidity." That's what negative peers are. Unfortunately, we find them not only amongst young people but we find them amongst older people, too....

In every high school, you have two groups: you have your nerds and you have your cool guys. Now many of you were probably nerds. I was. You can always *tell* the difference. Because the cool guys are the ones who have the latest fashions, they know all the popular tunes, they can talk about all the movies, they have lettered in sports, they have a car, they have three chicks on each arm. The nerd, on the other hand—his clothes are clean, he carries books (even outside the school), he has these big, thick glasses, and he even understands his science experiments. And none of the girls want to be seen talking to him in public....

But something happens. A few years go by. It's time to graduate from high school. Now the nerd wins a scholarship, goes off to college. The cool guy, with all his coolness, walks over to McDonald's and gets himself a job there. A few more years go by. The cool guy's still flipping hamburgers. The nerd has done very well, and there he is getting a signed contract with one of the Fortune 500 companies, and [he] takes that big signing bonus, first stop—he goes to the eye doctor. Gets rid of those thick glasses and gets a pair of contact lenses. Next stop—he goes to the tailor, gets himself some nice clothes. Next stop—he goes to the automobile dealer, gets himself a nice car. And then all those girls who wouldn't talk to him, they say, "Hey, don't I know you?" They won't talk to the guy at McDonald's anymore.

What I'm talking about here is delayed gratification. I'm talking about the ability to plan for the future. That's why we have these sophisticated minds....

After I was able to learn these kinds of lessons, things went very well. I was able to go through high school, go to Yale

University, on to the University of Michigan, to Johns Hopkins....

When I was chief resident at Johns Hopkins, we had the grand opening of the new neuroscience center. Hopkins is the modern birthplace of neurosurgery, so everybody who is *anybody* was there, including one of the fellows from Australia. He kept after me to come to Australia.... I said, "Australia? You've got to be kidding me!" I mean, I didn't *say* that to him, but that's what I was thinking. I mean, where's Australia? You dig a hole in the earth from Baltimore, you come out in Australia. I don't wanna to go there! And plus I [had] heard all these things about, you know, it was worse than South Africa, they had a whites-only policy. So I said, forget about this mess.

But it seemed like every time I turned around there was someone there saying, "G'day, mate, how you doin'?" Australians *everywhere*. Every time we turned on the TV, there was a special on about Australia. I told my wife, "The Lord wants us to go there." So we packed up our belongings, off we went to Australia, and you know something? Interestingly enough, the biggest problem we had was keeping up with all the dinner invitations! People were enormously friendly....

The reason the Lord wanted me to go there, I got so *much* experience. It was incredible, doing things. It was the only referral hospital in all of western Australia, so by the time I came back and joined the staff at Johns Hopkins, I knew how to do just about everything. So when the position of director of pediatric neurosurgery opened up, they gave me the position even at the age of thirty-three. People would come from all kinds of places with their young children to see Dr. Carson, chief of pediatric neurosurgery at Johns Hopkins. I would walk in the room and they would say, "When's Dr. Carson coming?" They couldn't imagine it was me. And I would say, "Well, I'm Dr. Carson," and they'd just about fall down and have a seizure....

I started doing all kinds of interesting things. But the reason I would do these operations—the hemispherectomies, the **intrauterine** surgery, separation of Siamese twins—I would ask myself the question, "What happens if I *don't* do

intrauterine: inside the womb.

it?" And if the answer was they're going to die or something horrible, I would say, "You've got nothing to lose." The fact of the matter is, if you do your best and let God do the rest, you don't have to worry about what's going to happen.

99

Sources

Books

Carson, Ben, with Cecil B. Murphey, *Gifted Hands: The Ben Carson Story,* Zondervan, 1990.

Carson, Ben, *Think Big: Unleashing Your Potential for Excellence,* Zondervan, 1992.

Periodicals

Black Enterprise, "Merging Medicine with Technology," October 1988, p. 70.

Christianity Today, "Surgeon on a Mission: With Prayer and Self-Discipline, Ben Carson Overcame Poverty to Become America's Leading Pediatric Neurosurgeon," May 27, 1991, pp. 24-26.

Ebony, "Surgical Superstar," January 1988, pp. 52-58; "The Love That Changed My Life," May 1990, p. 38.

People, "The Physician Who Healed Himself First," fall 1991 (special issue), pp. 96-99.

Reader's Digest, "Ben Carson: Man of Miracles," April 1990, pp. 71-75.

Other

Gifted Hands: The Ben Carson Story (video recording), Zondervan, 1992.

Gifted Hands (audio recording), Million Dollar Round Table Tape Cassette Program, 1994.

Think Big: Unleashing Your Potential for Excellence (audio recording), two cassettes, Audio Pages, 1992.

Shirley Chisholm

1924–

Politician and women's rights activist

In November 1968, Shirley Chisholm made history when she became the first black woman elected to the United States Congress. On January 25, 1972, she made history once again when she became the first black and the first woman to announce her intention to seek the Democratic presidential nomination. Although these are important "firsts," they are by no means Chisholm's only accomplishments as a politician and activist at both the state and national level. Her efforts to improve the lives of women and children—especially those trapped in poverty—have earned her widespread admiration and respect.

Early Life

Chisholm was born in Brooklyn, New York, but spent most of her early childhood on the Caribbean island of Barbados. There she lived with her maternal grandmother while her parents remained in the United States and worked to make a better life for the family. Young Shirley

"UNLESS WE START TO FIGHT AND DEFEAT THE ENEMIES OF POVERTY AND RACISM IN OUR OWN COUNTRY AND MAKE OUR TALK OF EQUALITY AND OPPORTUNITY RING TRUE, WE ARE EXPOSED AS HYPOCRITES IN THE EYES OF THE WORLD WHEN WE TALK ABOUT MAKING OTHER PEOPLE FREE."

attended the British-style schools on Barbados until she was about ten, at which time she rejoined her parents in New York City. After graduating from the public school system, Chisholm went on to study early childhood education and earned a bachelor's degree from Brooklyn College and a master's degree from Columbia University. She began her career as a teacher at a nursery school and eventually was promoted to director, a position she held for twenty years.

Chisholm became active in politics during the early 1950s when she worked mostly behind the scenes for the local Democratic party. By 1960, she was a key figure in her district's struggle to defeat several long-established politicians and develop a new team of leaders. Her own election to the New York State Assembly followed in 1964, and in 1968, she won a seat in the U.S. House of Representatives.

Makes Waves in Washington, D.C.

While serving at the state level, Chisholm had gained a reputation for being straightforward, spirited, and hardworking. She was also a fiercely independent woman who did not always do what her party leadership expected its members to do. In Washington, Chisholm continued to rock the boat. In a dramatic break with tradition, she refused to accept a post on the House Agricultural Committee and instead demanded an assignment that was more in line with her own interests and the needs of her constituents (the people who elect someone to public office to represent them). She eventually ended up on the Veterans' Affairs Committee and, later, the Education and Labor Committee.

On March 26, 1969, Chisholm delivered her first speech before fellow members of the House of Representatives. Richard Nixon had just taken office as president, following Lyndon Johnson, who had declined to run again. Despite the promise of a new administration, however, the country was in turmoil. Overseas, the United States was fighting a very unpopular war in Vietnam. At home, a variety of social and economic problems had people on edge. In her remarks, Chisholm made it clear that she felt it was time for a change in national priorities. Her speech is reprinted here from the Congressional Record, 91st Congress, 1st session, U.S. Government Printing Office, 1969.

"

Mr. Speaker, on the same day President Nixon announced he had decided the United States will not be safe unless we start to build a defense system against missiles, the Headstart program in the District of Columbia was cut back for the lack of money.

As a teacher, and as a woman, I do not think I will ever understand what kind of values can be involved in spending nine billion dollars—and more, I am sure—on elaborate, unnecessary and impractical weapons when several thousand disadvantaged children in the nation's capital get nothing.

When the new administration took office, I was one of the

many Americans who hoped it would mean that our country would benefit from the fresh perspectives, the new ideas, the different priorities of a leader who had no part in the mistakes of the past. Mr. Nixon had said things like this: "If our cities are to be livable for the next generation, we can delay no longer in launching new approaches to the problems that beset them and to the tensions that tear them apart." And he said, "When you cut expenditures for education, what you are doing is shortchanging the American future."

But frankly, I have never cared too much what people say. What I am interested in is what they do. We have waited to see what the new administration is going to do. The pattern now is becoming clear.

Apparently launching those new programs can be delayed for a while, after all. It seems we have to get some missiles launched first.

Recently the new Secretary of Commerce spelled it out. The secretary, Mr. [Maurice] Stans, told a reporter that the new administration is "pretty well agreed it must take time out from major social objectives" until it can stop inflation.

The new Secretary of Health, Education and Welfare, Robert Finch, came to the Hill to tell the House Education and Labor Committee that he thinks we should spend more on education, particularly in city schools. But, he said, unfortunately we cannot "afford" to, until we have reached some kind of honorable solution to the Vietnam war. I was glad to read that the distinguished Member from Oregon [Mrs. Green] asked Mr. Finch this: "With the crisis we have in education, and the crisis in our cities, can we wait to settle the war? Shouldn't it be the other way around? Unless we can meet the crisis in education, we really can't afford the war."

Secretary of Defense Melvin Laird came to Capitol Hill, too. His mission was to sell the **antiballistic-missile** insanity to the Senate. He was asked what the new administration is doing about the war. To hear him, one would have thought it was 1968, that the former secretary of state was defending the former policies, that nothing had ever happened—a president had never decided not to run because he knew the nation would reject him, in despair over this tragic war we

antiballistic-missile: a missile that stops and destroys air-borne rockets

Shirley Chisholm

have blundered into. Mr. Laird talked of being prepared to spend at least two more years in Vietnam.

Two more years, two more years of hunger for Americans, of death for our best young men, of children here at home suffering the lifelong handicap of not having a good education when they are young. Two more years of high taxes, collected to feed the cancerous growth of a Defense Department budget that now consumes two thirds of our federal income.

Two more years of too little being done to fight our greatest enemies, poverty, prejudice and neglect, here in our own country. Two more years of fantastic waste in the Defense Department and of penny pinching on social programs. Our country cannot survive two more years, or four, of these kinds of policies. It must stop—this year—now.

Now, I am not a pacifist. I am deeply, unalterably opposed to this war in Vietnam. Apart from all the other considerations—and they are many—the main fact is that we cannot squander there the lives, the money, the energy that we need desperately here, in our cities, in our schools.

I wonder whether we cannot reverse our whole approach to spending. For years, we have given the military, the defense industry, a blank check. New weapons systems are dreamed up, billions are spent, and many times they are found to be impractical, inefficient, unsatisfactory, even worthless. What do we do then? We spend more money on them. But with social programs, what do we do? Take the Job Corps. Its failure has been mercilessly exposed and criticized. If it had been a military research and development project, they would have been covered up or explained away, and Congress would have been ready to pour more billions after those that had been wasted on it....

We Americans have come to feel that it is our mission to make the world free. We believe that we are the good guys, everywhere—in Vietnam, in Latin America, wherever we go. We believe we are the good guys at home, too. When the Kerner Commission [see box] told white America what black America had always known, that prejudice and hatred built the nation's slums, maintain them and profit by them, white America would not believe it. But it is true. Unless we start to fight and defeat the enemies of poverty and racism in our own country and make our talk of equality and opportunity ring true, we are exposed as **hypocrites** in the eyes of the world when we talk about making other people free.

I am deeply disappointed at the clear evidence that the number-one priority of the new administration is to buy

hypocrites: people who claim to have high moral standards but who do not really live by them.

The Kerner Commission

During the summer of 1967, the United States experienced the worst summer of racial disturbances in its history. More than forty riots broke out in cities across the country, including Newark, New Jersey; Detroit, Michigan; New York City; Cleveland, Ohio; Washington, D.C.; Chicago, Illinois; and Atlanta, Georgia. Later that same year, President Lyndon Johnson brought together outstanding leaders from all walks of life to form the National Advisory Commission on Civil Disorders, which came to be known as the Kerner Commission after its chairman, Governor Otto Kerner of Illinois. This special group was asked to discover what had led to all the violence and what should be done to prevent future trouble.

After a series of hearings and other investigations, the commission issued a report on its findings in the spring of 1968. The Kerner Report, as it was called, created a stir with its declaration that "white racism" was the major cause of the 1967 riots. It also stated that the country was in danger of splitting into two separate societies, "one white, one black, separate and unequal."

more and more weapons of war, to return to the era of the cold war, to ignore the war we must fight here—the war that is not optional. There is only one way, I believe, to turn these policies around. The Congress can respond to the mandate that the American people have clearly expressed. They have said, "End this war. Stop the waste. Stop the killing. Do something for your own people first." We must find the money to "launch the new approaches," as Mr. Nixon said. We must force the administration to rethink its distorted, unreal scale of priorities. Our children, our jobless men, our deprived, rejected and starving fellow citizens must come first.

For this reason, I intend to vote "No" on every money bill that comes to the floor of this House that provides any funds for the Department of Defense. Any bill whatsoever, until the time comes when our values and priorities have been turned right side up again, until the monstrous waste and the shocking profits in the defense budget have been eliminated and our country starts to use its strength, its tremendous resources, for people and peace, not for profits and war.

It was Calvin Coolidge, I believe, who made the comment that "the Business of America is Business." We are now spending eighty billion dollars a year on defense—that is two-thirds of every tax dollar. At this time, gentlemen, the business of America is war, and it is time for a change.

99

As a member of Congress, Chisholm worked tirelessly on issues involving women, children, education, and what she saw as the government's neglect of minorities—all minorities, not just blacks. In January 1972, she decided to take her message to a national audience as the first black and the first woman to run for the Democratic presidential nomination. The theme of many of her campaign speeches that year was economic injustice in America. In her travels across the country, she discussed her views on the unequal treatment and opportunities experienced by most of the country's minorities. She also proposed how she would change things for the better.

Chisholm emphasized again and again during her campaign that she was "the candidate of the people" and not just the candidate of black America or the candidate of women's groups. Nevertheless, her quest for the nomination took on symbolic meaning for African Americans and women. As a result, she never really managed to broaden her support and become a "real" candidate in the eyes of most voters. She was also never able to win over members of the Congressional Black Caucus, an influential group of black congressmen. Many of them viewed her as a self-serving troublemaker, believing that she had only made it more difficult for them to promote black male politicians. Thus, in July 1972, it was South Dakota Senator George McGovern who won the Democratic presidential nomination. He was then trounced by President Nixon in the November election.

Chisholm remained in Congress until 1982, when she decided to retire for a combination of personal and political reasons. She has remained very active in public life, however. She lectures extensively, has taught political science and women's studies at the college level, and works on behalf of various political causes. In 1984 and again in 1988, for example, she lent her expertise and support to Jesse

Jackson's run for the Democratic presidential nomination. And in the mid-1980s, she co-founded the National Political Congress of Black Women, an organization dedicated to advancing civil rights and social programs. In 1993, President Bill Clinton asked Chisholm to serve as his ambassador to Jamaica, but she declined due to eye problems that had left her with poor vision.

Sources

Books

Braden, Waldo W., editor, *Representative American Speeches: 1971-1972,* Wilson, 1972.

Braden, Waldo W., editor, *Representative American Speeches: 1972-1973,* Wilson, 1973.

Brownmiller, Susan, *Shirley Chisholm: A Biography,* Doubleday, 1970.

Chisholm, Shirley, *Unbought and Unbossed,* Houghton, 1970.

Chisholm, Shirley, *The Good Fight,* Harper, 1973.

Congressional Record, 91st Congress, 1st session, U.S. Government Printing Office, 1969.

Duffy, Bernard K., and Halford R. Ryan, editors, *American Orators of the Twentieth Century: Critical Studies and Sources,* Greenwood Press, 1987.

Haskins, James, *Fighting Shirley Chisholm,* Dial, 1975.

Eldridge Cleaver

1935–
Political and social activist

> "I KNOW THAT IN YOUR EDUCATION YOU WERE GIVEN TO BELIEVE THE MELTING POT THEORY.... BUT IN THIS STEW THAT'S BEEN PRODUCED BY THESE YEARS AND YEARS OF STIRRING THE POT, YOU'LL FIND THAT THE BLACK ELEMENTS ... HAVE NOT BLENDED WELL WITH THE REST OF THE INGREDIENTS."

Among the best-known black figures on the national scene during the late 1960s was Eldridge Cleaver. He was the so-called "Minister of Information" for the radical Black Panther Party. In this role, he helped shape the Panthers' militant philosophy of black nationalism and made sure their message reached as many people as possible. To achieve this goal, Cleaver skillfully used both the written and spoken word.

Early Life

Cleaver was born near Little Rock, Arkansas, and later moved with his parents to Los Angeles, California. He spent much of the 1950s and early 1960s as an inmate in various state prisons. His crimes ranged from theft and drug dealing and he was charged with assault with intent to kill for raping several white women.

Eventually, Cleaver made up his mind to follow a different path in life. He finished his high school education in prison and concentrated on developing his writing skills. He then began working on the provocative essays that would later make him so famous. While he was in prison, Cleaver also converted to the Black Muslim faith. After the assassination of **Malcolm X** *(see entry), however, he broke his ties to the Nation of Islam.*

Joins the Black Panthers

In 1967, Cleaver joined the Black Panthers (see box). Besides serving as the party's minister of information, he was editor of its newspaper, The Black Panther. *In his writings for this publication as well as in his speeches, Cleaver showed again and again that he was willing to take the black revolution in new directions.*

For example, he proposed holding a vote—to be supervised by the United Nations—to determine whether blacks wanted to remain part of the United States. And unlike many of his fellow Panthers, he supported the idea of forming a **coalition** *with white radicals, specifically the group known as the Peace and Freedom Party. By working together, he said, they could more effectively challenge the forces of oppression. (To the Panthers and many others in the black and radical community, the police were the major symbols of this oppression.) Cleaver was so committed to making a success of this coalition that in 1968 he even ran for president of the United States as a candidate of the Peace and Freedom Party.*

These and other causes Cleaver championed generated controversy both inside and outside the Black Panther Party. His ideas reached a widespread audience in 1968, when he published his best-selling book, Soul on Ice, *a collection of essays on his own life and black attitudes toward American society.*

In its March 16, 1968, issue, The Black Panther *included the text of a speech Cleaver had given outlining his views on the political struggle in America and why it was so important to establish ties with white radicals. It was later reprinted in the book* Rhetoric of Black Revolution, *by Arthur L. Smith, Allyn & Bacon, 1969. The following excerpt of Cleaver's speech is taken from that book.*

coalition: an alliance of different people or groups who come together to take action.

The Black Panthers

During the late 1960s, one of the most visible and most feared **black nationalist** groups in America was the Black Panther Party for Self-Defense, popularly known as the Black Panthers. The party was formed in Oakland, California, in October 1966 by two young black activists, Huey Newton and Bobby Seale. Most of their inspiration came from the teachings of Malcolm X and from **communist** thinkers such as Germany's Karl Marx and Friedrich Engels, Russia's Vladimir Lenin, China's Mao Zedong, and Vietnam's Ho Chi Minh. Cuban guerrilla leader Che Guevara was also one of their heroes.

The Black Panthers expressed their belief that only a true revolution—both economic and social—could bring about the kinds of changes needed to overcome the effects of white oppression in the black community. They also demanded an end to police brutality and declared that blacks would take up arms to protect themselves against such violence.

The Black Panthers maintained their militant image by taking on a deliberately fierce appearance. They typically wore "uniforms" consisting of black berets and black leather jackets, with guns and ammunition clips slung over their shoulders and their eyes hidden behind black sunglasses. Their look and manner frightened many Americans, especially whites, which led to violent and often deadly police crackdowns on the Black Panthers and their sympathizers. By the early 1970s, most of the group's leaders were dead, in prison, under arrest, or on the run from the authorities.

black nationalist: a member of a group of people who believe that blacks should separate from whites and form their own self-governing communities and businesses.

communist: characterized by a belief in communism, an economic system in which the government (rather than private individuals or companies) owns and controls the means of producing goods, which are then supposed to be shared by everyone equally.

dynamics: forces or patterns of change and growth.

homogeneous: of the same or similar type (not showing any variety of races, for example).

I think the first thing we have to realize ... is that it is a reality when you hear people say that there's a "black colony" and a "white mother country." I think you really have to get that distinction clear in your minds in order to understand that there are two different sets of political **dynamics** functioning in this country.... For instance, if there's a **homogeneous** country and everyone here is a citizen of that country, when it comes to participating in the politics of this country, it makes a lot of sense to insist that black people participate in electoral politics and all the other forms of politics as we have known them. But if you accept the analysis that the black colony is separate and distinct from the mother country, then a lot of other forms of political struggle are indicated.

I think that most black revolutionaries or militants or what have you have generally accepted this distinction. A lot of people seem reluctant to accept this distinction. I know that in your education you were given to believe the melting pot theory, that people have come from all over the world and they've been put into this big pot and they've been melted into American citizens. In terms of the white immigrants who came to this country, this is more or less true. But in this stew that's been produced by these years and years of stirring the pot, you'll find that the black elements, the black components, have not blended well with the rest of the ingredients. And this is so because of the forms of oppression that have been generated—black people have been blocked out of this, and blocked out of that, and not allowed to participate in this, and excluded from that. This has created a psychology in black people where they have now turned all the negative exclusions to their advantage.

[By this] I mean the same things that were used to our disadvantage are now being turned around to our advantage. The whole thing about condemning blackness and developing an inferior image of everything black has now been turned completely around.... I think the slogan of Black Power was a recognition of the change in the psychology of black people, that in fact they have seized upon their blackness and rallied around the elements or the points at which they were oppressed. They have turned the focal point of the oppression into the focal point of the struggle for national liberation.

Now, when people decide in their own minds that they are going to separate themselves from a country or from a political situation, a lot of dynamics and a lot of directions flow from that basic distinction. For example, people are talking these days about going to the United Nations and seeking membership in the United Nations for Afro-America. And when you look at the **criteria** for nationhood, you'll find that the only place that black people fall short in terms of this standard is the one where the land question comes up.... Now, that land question was a hang-up for a long time, simply because the black people in this country were **dispersed** throughout the population of the mother country. People couldn't begin to deal with the question of how to build a nation on someone else's land....

In the history of the liberation struggle in this country, the two outstanding efforts that we remember in history were

criteria: rules; standards on which judgements are based.

dispersed: scattered.

the **Marcus Garvey** [see entry] movement and the Nation of Islam under Elijah Muhammad [see **Malcolm X** entry]. I consider their fundamental mistake was that they projected goals that they were unable to fulfill....

The beautiful thing about the slogan "Black Power" was that it **implemented** the **dictum** laid down by Kwame Nkrumah [an African politician who helped gain Ghana's independence from Great Britain], in which he said, "Seek ye first the political kingdom, and other things will be added unto you." It's very important to realize that in moving to gain power, you do not conceal or **repudiate** the land question, you hold it in **abeyance.** What you're saying is that we must first get ourselves organized, and then we can get some of this land....

I think it's very important to realize that there is a way to move. So that today black people are talking about ... asking the United Nations for a UN-supervised **plebiscite** throughout the colony. Black people have never been able through any mechanism to express what their will is. People have come along and spoken in the name of black people; they have said that black people want to be integrated; they have said black people want to be separated; but no where at no time have black people been given the chance to register their own position. I think it's very important that we decide this once and for all, because as black people we are able to wage a campaign on this subject: do you want to be a part of America, do you want to be integrated into America, or do you want to be separated from America...? I think it would be very hard for the black people to say no, particularly when the argument of the government is going to be that black people don't need those things because they are already American citizens. Because then we come back and say, Well, if we're citizens, what about this, and what about that? And, at the very least, what it will do is to put tremendous pressure on the [whites], and they need all the pressure we can give them.

Now, a lot of people don't want to see this country and its structure basically change. They want to think the United States of America is an eternal **entity.** When you look at history, you'll find that great empires have had their boundaries changed, have had their political structures rearranged [over the years].... You will find that a day of **reckoning** came

implemented: put into effect.

dictum: a formal pronouncement of a key principle or belief.

repudiate: reject.

abeyance: a temporary state of inactivity.

plebiscite: vote.

entity: being, thing.

reckoning: judgment.

Black Panther cofounders Bobby Seale (left) and Huey Newton, 1969

down and the whole situation was rearranged. Americans cannot envision a situation where the same thing could happen here. I think that black people have already envisioned that this, in fact, could happen....

One thing about the coalition with the Peace and Freedom Party [of white radicals]: we approached this whole thing from the point of view of international relations. We feel that our coalition is part of our foreign policy. That is how we look at it, that is how we are moving on it and thinking about it.

A lot of people feel ... we are endangering them as well as ourselves by **coalescing** with the white radicals, particularly here in Berkeley [a university town in California that was a major center of student radicalism during the 1960s]. Berke-

coalescing: merging, cooperating.

ley, as far as we can see, has a foul reputation among a lot of black cats....

We recognize that we have a powerful interest in seeing a white radical movement develop into something that we can relate to. There are many things that we cannot do by ourselves. And then, there are many things that the white radical movement cannot do by itself. So we recognize that, and we are not going to be running around trying to stab each other in the back....

Now, one very important thing that we are working towards is how to unify the black population in this country within a national structure. The structure has to be inclusive enough to pull in all black people. In the past, when a new organization came on the scene, it sought to eliminate existing organizations.... We say that this is a mistake. What we have done is worked out a merger with SNCC [Student Non-violent Coordinating Committee]....

It is very important to realize that SNCC is composed virtually of black hippies, you might say, of black college students who have dropped out of the black middle class. And because that is their origin and that is where they came from, they cannot relate to the black brother on the block in a political fashion. They can relate to him, they can talk to him, they can communicate with him much better than, say, **Roy Wilkins** [see entry] ever could. But, they are not able to move him **en masse** to the point where he could be organized and involved in political functions....

Now, we have done two important things, I think. One, we have made this coalition with the Peace and Freedom Party; and two, we have merged with SNCC. When people look at that they can say that in the Era of Black Power, we have got to merge and merge into larger units until we have a national structure. In terms of our relationship with the white community, we can move with functional coalitions.

It is very important that we [the Black Panthers and the Peace and Freedom Party] all hold up our end of the bargain—and don't think that by using us you can get away with something, because, in fact, you will only destroy what you are trying to build for yourself. Black people have only one way to protect themselves, particularly politically, and

en masse: as a group.

that is to be capable of implementing and inflicting a political consequence. If we cannot inflict a political consequence, then we will in fact become nothing. So, that if the Peace and Freedom Party ever tries to misuse us, we have to be in a position to hurt the Peace and Freedom Party....

We are also catching a lot of hell—the word is **purgatory,** rather, it is not hell—about this coalition. Because a lot of people have begun to feel that we can be trusted, they have taken a wait-and-see attitude to find out how this coalition comes down, to see if we, in fact, do become puppets [of the white radicals]....

I think we have a good thing going. I want to see it continue to develop and broaden and deepen because we are all involved in this and there is no way out. We have got to do it, because time is against us, a lot of people are against us, and I know that I am out of time, so I think I will cool it right here.

"

*Cleaver's life since the heyday of the Black Panthers has taken several unusual twists and turns. During the early 1970s, for example, he went into **exile** overseas to avoid being sent back to prison for his role in a 1968 shootout between the Black Panthers and police in Oakland, California. When he finally returned to the United States in 1975, Cleaver surprised many people by announcing that he had become a born-again Christian, a process he describes in his 1978 book* Soul on Fire. *Then, during the 1980s, he proudly declared himself to be a Republican and noted that he had cast his vote for Ronald Reagan as president. Cleaver has also tried his hand at a number of business ventures, including fashion design and running a recycling service.*

In contrast to these activities are Cleaver's continuing difficulties with the law. In 1988, he was convicted of burglary and put on probation. Later that same year, he was jailed for violating the terms of his probation when he tested positive for cocaine use.

*Cleaver entered a drug **rehabilitation** program in 1990 for what he said was an addiction to crack cocaine. Events after that time suggest it is a problem he did not*

exile: (a period of absence from one's country or home).

purgatory: a place of temporary suffering (as opposed to the permanent suffering of hell).

rehabilitation: the act of restoring to good health and a productive life.

manage to overcome. In 1992, he was arrested for posses-
sion of crack, but the charges against him were eventually
dropped because police had found the drug during an ille-
gal search. Two years later, Cleaver was arrested for
alleged *public drunkenness and possession of cocaine and*
drug ***paraphernalia.*** *He then had to undergo emergency*
surgery for a brain ***hemorrhage*** *after suddenly becoming*
ill at the police station.

In early 1996, at the invitation of a longtime friend who
runs a Christian center, Cleaver moved to Miami, Florida.
There he strove to stay away from drugs and get his life
back on track through Bible study, writing, lecturing, and a
renewed commitment to political and social activism.
Cleaver regularly shared his message with audiences at
local schools, jails, and juvenile halls. He also hit the road
occasionally to speak at colleges and universities, often
with another former Black Panther, Bobby Seale.

Sources

Books

Cleaver, Eldridge, *Soul on Ice,* McGraw, 1968.

Cleaver, Eldridge, *Soul on Fire,* Word Inc., 1978.

Foner, Philip S., editor, *The Black Panthers Speak,* Lippincott, 1970.

Holland, DeWitte, editor, *America in Controversy: History of American Public Address,* William C. Brown Company, 1973.

Scheer, Robert, editor, *Eldridge Cleaver: Post-Prison Writings and Speeches,* Random House, 1969.

Smith, Arthur L., *Rhetoric of Black Revolution,* Allyn & Bacon, 1969.

Smith, Arthur L., and Stephen Robb, editors, *The Voice of Black Rhetoric: Selections,* Allyn & Bacon, 1971.

Periodicals

Detroit News, "Children of the Revolution," August 13, 1995.

People, "Free at Last," April 15, 1996, pp. 79-80.

alleged: claimed, charged.

paraphernalia: equipment, supplies.

hemorrhage: an episode of heavy and uncontrollable bleeding.

Frederick Douglass

1817–1895

Antislavery activist, journalist, and United States government official

Frederick Douglass was the most famous and influential black leader of the entire nineteenth century. An eloquent speaker whose striking physical appearance enhanced his message, he brought great intelligence and passion to the national debate over slavery. This combination of qualities made him one of the country's foremost antislavery activists in the years leading up to the Civil War.

Early Life

Douglass was born into slavery on a plantation in Talbot County, Maryland, around 1817. He spent much of his youth as a house servant in Baltimore. There he learned to read and write before he was sent back to the plantation to work as a field hand.

The cruel treatment Douglass was then forced to endure strengthened his determination to escape, and in 1838 he fled to freedom in New York City. From there he made his way to Massachusetts, home of the well-known **abolitionist** William Lloyd Garrison and his Antislavery Society.

"WHAT, TO THE AMERICAN SLAVE, IS YOUR 4TH OF JULY? I ANSWER; A DAY THAT REVEALS TO HIM, MORE THAN ALL OTHER DAYS IN THE YEAR, THE GROSS INJUSTICE AND CRUELTY TO WHICH HE IS THE CONSTANT VICTIM."

Achieves Fame as Lecturer and Editor

Douglass's quick mind and skill at public speaking were so impressive that he soon became the Antislavery Society's chief spokesperson. Beginning in 1847, he also gained fame as the founder and editor of the North Star *newspaper. In its pages, besides campaigning against slavery, he advocated equal rights for women and Native Americans, supported public education, and opposed the death penalty.*

*Douglass's widespread reputation sprang mainly from his fiery yet carefully thought-out arguments calling for an end to slavery. His speeches left no doubt as to the depth of his hatred for the system that had imprisoned him and his fellow blacks. Perhaps his strongest and most bitterly **ironic** condemnation of slavery came in an address he gave in Rochester, New York, on July 5, 1852. The event was in honor of America's Independence Day, so Douglass's speech is often called his "Fourth of July Oration." In it, he blasts the **hypocrisy** of a nation that celebrates freedom while enslaving millions. An excerpt from the very long speech he gave that day is reprinted here from* Rhetoric of Black Revolution *by Arthur L. Smith, Allyn & Bacon, 1969.*

❝

...**The distance between this platform and the slave plantation, from which I escaped, is considerable—** and the difficulties to be overcome in getting from the latter to the former are by no means slight. That I am here to-day is, to me, a matter of astonishment as well as of gratitude....

This, for the purpose of this celebration, is the Fourth of July. It is the birthday of your national independence, and of your political freedom.... This celebration also marks the beginning of another year of your national life; and reminds you that the Republic of America is now 76 years old. I am glad, fellow-citizens, that your nation is so young. Seventy-six years, though a good old age for a man, is but a mere speck in the life of a nation.... According to this fact, you are, even now, only in the beginning of your national career, still lingering in the period of childhood.... There is hope in the thought, and hope is much needed, under the dark clouds which lower

abolitionist: a person in favor of getting rid of, or abolishing, slavery.

ironic: sarcastically saying one thing when the opposite is actually true.

hypocrisy: expressing high moral standards but not living by them.

above the horizon. The eye of the reformer is met with angry flashes, **portending** disastrous times; but his heart may well beat lighter at the thought that America is young, and that she is still in the impressible stage of her existence....

Friends and citizens, I need not enter further into the causes which led to this anniversary. Many of you understand them better than I do....

My business, if I have any here today, is with the present.... We have to do with the past only as we can make it useful to the present and to the future.... Now is the time, the important time. Your fathers have lived, died, and have done their work, and have done much of it well. You live and must die, and you must do your work.....

Fellow-citizens, pardon me, allow me to ask, why am I called upon to speak here today? What have I, or those I represent, to do with your national independence? Are the great principles of political freedom and of natural justice, embodied in that Declaration of Independence, extended to us? And am I, therefore, called upon to bring our humble offering to the national altar, and to confess the benefits and express devout gratitude for the blessings resulting from your independence to us?

Would to God, both for your sakes and ours, that an **affirmative answer** could be truthfully returned to these questions! Then would my task be light, and my burden easy and delightful....

But such is not the state of the case. I say it with a sad sense of the **disparity** between us. I am not included within the **pale** of this glorious anniversary! Your high independence only reveals the immeasurable distance between us. The blessings in which you, this day, rejoice, are not enjoyed in common. The rich inheritance of justice, liberty, prosperity and independence, **bequeathed** by your fathers, is shared by you, not by me. The sunlight that brought light and healing to you, has brought stripes and death to me. This Fourth of July is *yours,* not *mine. You* may rejoice, I must mourn. To drag a man in **fetters** into the grand illuminated temple of liberty, and call upon him to join you in joyous anthems, were inhuman mockery and **sacrilegious irony....**

portending: warning, forecasting.

affirmative answer: a "yes" answer.

disparity: contrast, difference.

pale: boundaries.

bequeathed: passed down, left.

fetters: chains, shackles.

sacrilegious irony: corruption of a sacred idea (in this case, liberty) by saying or doing one thing when the opposite is actually true.

Fellow-citizens, above your national, tumultuous joy, I hear the mournful wail of millions! Whose chains, heavy and grievous yesterday, are, today, **rendered** more intolerable by the jubilee shouts that reach them.... To forget them, to pass lightly over their wrongs, and to chime in with the popular theme, would be treason most scandalous and shocking, and would make me a reproach disgrace before God and the world. My subject, then, fellow-citizens, is AMERICAN SLAVERY. I shall see this day and its popular characteristics from the slave's point of view. Standing there identified with the American **bondman,** making his wrongs mine, I do not hesitate to declare, with all my soul, that the character and conduct of this nation never looked blacker to me than on this 4th of July! Whether we turn to the declarations of the past, or to the **professions** of the present, the conduct of the nation seems equally hideous and revolting. America is false to the past, false to the present, and solemnly binds herself to be false to the future. Standing with God and the crushed and bleeding slave on this occasion, I will, in the name of humanity which is outraged, in the name of liberty which is fettered, in the name of the Constitution and the Bible which are disregarded and trampled upon, dare to call in question and to denounce, with all the emphasis I can command, everything that serves to **perpetuate** slavery—the great sin and shame of America!...

Had I the ability, and could I reach the nation's ear, I would, today, pour out a fiery stream of biting ridicule, blasting reproach, withering sarcasm, and stern rebuke. For it is not light that is needed, but fire; it is not the gentle shower, but thunder. We need the storm, the whirlwind, and the earthquake. The feeling of the nation must be quickened; the conscience of the nation must be roused; the **propriety** of the nation must be startled; the hypocrisy of the nation must be exposed; and its crimes against God and man must be proclaimed and denounced.

What, to the American slave, is your 4th of July? I answer; a day that reveals to him, more than all other days in the year, the gross injustice and cruelty to which he is the constant victim. To him, your celebration is a **sham;** your boasted liberty, an unholy **license;** your national greatness, swelling vanity; your sounds of rejoicing are empty and heartless; your denun-

rendered: made.

bondman: slave.

professions: open declarations of belief in and loyalty to certain principles.

perpetuate: continue.

propriety: sense of what is correct or right.

sham: hoax.

license: freedom.

ciation of tyrants, brass-fronted **impudence;** your shouts of liberty and equality, hollow mockery; your prayers and hymns, your sermons and thanksgivings, with all your religious parade and solemnity, are to Him, mere **bombast,** fraud, deception, **impiety,** and hypocrisy—a thin veil to cover up crimes which would disgrace a nation of savages. There is not a nation on the earth guilty of practices more shocking and bloody than are the people of the United States, at this very hour....

Take the American slave-trade, which we are told by the papers, is especially prosperous just now.... This trade is one of the peculiarities of American institutions. It is carried on in all the large towns and cities in one-half of this confederacy; and millions are pocketed every year by dealers in this horrid traffic. In several states this trade is a chief source of wealth.... The men engaged in the slave-trade between the states pass without condemnation, and their business is deemed honorable....

Behold the practical operation of this internal slave-trade, the American slave-trade, sustained by American politics and American religion. Here you will see men and women reared like **swine** for the market. You know what is a swine-drover? I will show you a man-drover. They inhabit all our Southern states. They **perambulate** the country, and crowd the highways of the nation, with droves of human stock. You will see one of these human flesh jobbers, armed with pistol, whip, and bowie-knife, driving a company of a hundred men, women, and children, from the Potomac to the slave market at New Orleans.... Mark the sad procession, as it moves wearily along, and the inhuman wretch who drives them. Hear his savage yells and his blood-curdling oaths, as he hurries on his **affrighted** captives!... Follow this drove to New Orleans. Attend the auction; see men examined like horses; see the forms of women rudely and brutally exposed to the shocking gaze of American slave-buyers. See this drove sold and separated forever; and never forget the deep, sad sobs that arose from that scattered multitude. Tell me, citizens, WHERE, under the sun, you can witness a spectacle more fiendish and shocking. Yet this is but a glance at the American slave-trade, as it exists, at this moment....

I was born amid such sights and scenes. To me the American slave-trade is a terrible reality....

impudence: boldness, brashness.

bombast: overblown speech or writing.

impiety: lack of proper respect or reverence.

swine: hogs.

perambulate: travel across or throughout.

affrighted: frightened, terrified.

Slave auction, Charleston, 1861

But a still more inhuman, disgraceful, and scandalous state of things remains to be presented.

By an act of the American Congress, not yet two years old, slavery has been nationalized in its most horrible and revolting form. [Douglass was probably referring here to the famous Compromise of 1850, which was designed to solve disputes between Northern abolitionists and Southern slaveholders over the question of slavery in the new U.S. territories in the West. Under the terms of the Compromise, slavery was outlawed in Washington, D.C., but allowed to remain in place everywhere else. In addition, California was admitted to the Union as a free state. Part of the Compromise was a tougher Fugitive Slave Law that made it easier to recover runaway slaves.] By that act, Mason and Dixon's line has been obliterated; New York has become as Virginia; and the power to hold, hunt, and sell men, women and children, as slaves, remains no longer a mere state institution, but is now an institution of the whole United States.... For black men there is neither law nor justice, humanity nor religion....

I take this law to be one of the grossest **infringements** of

infringements: violations.

Christian liberty, and, if the churches and ministers of our country were not stupidly blind, or most wickedly indifferent, they, too, would so regard it....

The church of this country is not only indifferent to the wrongs of the slave, it actually takes sides with the oppressors. It has made itself the **bulwark** of American slavery, and the shield of American slave-hunters. Many of its most eloquent Divines, who stand as the very lights of the church, have shamelessly given the **sanction** of religion and the Bible to the whole slave system....

For my part, I would say, welcome **infidelity!** Welcome **atheism!** Welcome anything in preference to the gospel, *as preached by those Divines!* They convert the very name of religion into an engine of tyranny and barbarous cruelty.... These ministers make religion a cold and flinty-hearted thing, having neither principles of right action nor bowels of compassion. They strip the love of God of its beauty and leave the throne of religion a huge, horrible, repulsive form. It is a religion for oppressors, tyrants, man-stealers, and *thugs....* [It is] a religion which favors the rich against the poor; which **exalts** the proud above the humble; which divides mankind into two classes, tyrants and slaves; which says to the man in chains, *stay there;* and to the oppressor, *oppress on;* it is a religion which may be professed and enjoyed by all the robbers and enslavers of mankind; it makes God a respecter of persons, denies his fatherhood of the race, and tramples in the dust the great truth of the brotherhood of man. All this we **affirm** to be true of the popular church, and the popular worship of our land and

bulwark: support, protection.

sanction: official permission or approval.

infidelity: faithlessness.

atheism: rejection of the belief in God.

exalts: gives a sense of greater importance to.

affirm: declare positively.

nation–a religion, a church, and a worship which, on the authority of inspired wisdom, we pronounce to be an **abomination** in the sight of God....

Let the religious press, the pulpit, the Sunday school, the conference meeting, the great ecclesiastical, missionary, Bible and tract associations of the land **array** their immense powers against slavery, and slave-holding; and the whole system of crime and blood would be scattered to the winds, and that they do not do this involves them in the most awful responsibility of which the mind can conceive....

There are exceptions, and I thank God that there are. Noble men may be found, scattered all over these Northern states...; and let me say further, that, upon these men lies the duty to inspire our ranks with high religious faith and zeal, and to cheer us on in the great mission of the slave's redemption from his chains....

Americans! Your republican politics, not less than your republican union, are **flagrantly inconsistent.** You boast of your love of liberty, your superior civilization, and your pure Christianity, which the whole political power of the nation (as embodied in the two great political parties) is solemnly pledged to support and perpetuate the enslavement of three millions of your countrymen.

You hurl your **anathemas** at the crowned headed tyrants of Russia and Austria and pride yourselves on your democratic institutions, while you yourselves consent to be the mere *tools* and *bodyguards* of the tyrants of Virginia and Carolina. You invite to your shores fugitives of oppression from abroad, honor them with banquets, greet them with ovations, cheer them, toast them, salute them, protect them, and pour out your money to them like water; but the fugitives from your own land you advertise, hunt, arrest, shoot, and kill.

You glory in your refinement and your universal education; yet you maintain a system as barbarous and dreadful as ever stained the character of a nation—a system begun in **avarice,** supported in pride, and perpetuated in cruelty.

You shed tears over fallen Hungary, and make the sad story of her wrongs the theme of your poets, statesmen, and orators, till your gallant sons are ready to fly to arms to **vindicate** her cause against the oppressor; but, in regard to the ten

abomination: something that provokes extreme disgust and hatred.

array: arrange, group.

flagrantly inconsistent: obviously or outrageously contradictory.

anathemas: curses.

avarice: greed.

vindicate: justify.

Frederick Douglass

thousand wrongs of the American slave, you would enforce the strictest silence, and would hail him as an enemy of the nation who dares to make those wrongs the subject of public **discourse!**

You are all on fire at the mention of liberty for France or for Ireland; but are as cold as an iceberg at the thought of liberty for the enslaved of America.

You discourse eloquently on the dignity of labor; yet, you sustain a system which, in its very essence, casts a **stigma** upon labor.

You can bare your bosom to the storm of British artillery to throw off a three-penny tax on tea; and yet wring the last

Engraving of a northerner returning an escaped slave to his southern slavemaster

discourse: conversation, discussion.
stigma: a mark of shame.

hard earned **farthing** from the grasp of the black laborers of your country.

You profess to believe "that, of one blood, God made all nations of men to dwell on the face of all the earth," and hath commanded all men, everywhere, to love one another; yet you notoriously hate (and glory in your hatred) all men whose skins are not colored like your own.

You declare before the world, and are understood by the world to declare that you *"hold these truths to be self evident, that all men are created equal; and are endowed by their Creator with certain inalienable rights; and that among these are, life, liberty, and the pursuit of happiness;"* and yet, you hold securely, in a bondage which, according to your own Thomas Jefferson, *"is worse than ages of that which your fathers rose in rebellion to oppose,"* a seventh part of the inhabitants of your country.

Fellow-citizens, I will not enlarge further on your national inconsistencies. The existence of slavery in this country brands your republicanism as a sham, your humanity as a **base pretense,** and your Christianity as a lie. It destroys your moral power abroad: it corrupts your politicians at home. It **saps** the foundation of religion; it makes your name a **hissing** and a bye-word to a mocking earth. It is the antagonistic force in your government, the only thing that seriously disturbs and endangers your *Union.* It fetters your progress; it is the enemy of improvement; the deadly foe of education; it fosters pride, it breeds **insolence;** it promotes vice; it shelters crime; it is a curse to the earth that supports it; and yet you cling to it as if it were the sheet anchor of all your hopes. Oh! Be warned! A horrible reptile is coiled up in your nation's bosom; the venomous creature is nursing at the tender breast of your youthful republic; *for the love of God, tear away,* and fling from you the hideous monster, and *let the weight of twenty millions crush and destroy it forever!*

But it is answered in reply to all this, that precisely what I have now denounced is, in fact, guaranteed and sanctioned by the Constitution of the United States; that, the right to hold, and to hunt slaves is a part of that Constitution framed by the illustrious Fathers of this Republic....

But I differ from those who charge this baseness on the framers of the Constitution of the United States. *It is a slander*

farthing: an old British coin worth less than a penny.

base pretense: worthless and false claim.

saps: undermines, weakens.

hissing: a target of sharp disapproval (that might be expressed by a hiss).

insolence: contempt, boldness.

Frederick Douglass

upon their memory, at least, so I believe. There is not time now to argue the constitutional question at length; nor have I the ability to discuss it as it ought to be discussed....

Fellow-citizens! There is no matter in respect to which the people of the North have allowed themselves to be so ruinously imposed upon as that of the pro-slavery character of the Constitution. In *that* instrument I hold there is neither **warrant,** license, nor sanction of the hateful thing; but interpreted, as it *ought* to be interpreted, the Constitution is a GLORIOUS LIBERTY DOCUMENT. Read its preamble, consider its purposes. Is slavery among them?... While I

do not intend to argue this question on the present occasion, let me ask, if it be not somewhat **singular** that, if the Constitution were intended to be, by its framers and adopters, a slaveholding instrument, why neither *slavery, slaveholding,* nor *slave* can anywhere be found in it....

Allow me to say, in conclusion, **notwithstanding** the dark picture I have this day presented, of the state of the nation, I do not despair of this country. There are forces in operation which must inevitably work the downfall of slavery.... I, therefore, leave off where I began, with *hope.* While drawing encouragement from "the Declaration of Independence," the great principles it contains, and the genius of American institutions, my spirit is also cheered by the obvi-

warrant: permission.
singular: odd.
notwithstanding: despite.

ous tendencies of the age. Nations do not now stand in the same relation to each other that they did ages ago. No nation can now shut itself up from the surrounding world and trot round in the same old path of its fathers without interference....

No abuse, no outrage whether in taste, sport or avarice, can now hide itself from the all-pervading light.... In the fervent aspirations of William Lloyd Garrison, I say, and let every heart join in saying it:

God speed the year of jubilee
The wide world o'er!
When from their galling chains set free,
Th' oppress'd shall vilely bend the knee,
And wear the yoke of tyranny
Like brutes no more.
That year will come, and freedom's reign,
To man his plundered rights again
Restore.

God speed the day when human blood
Shall cease to flow!
In every clime be understood,
The claims of human brotherhood,
And each return for evil, good,
Not blow for blow;
That day will come all feuds to end,
And change into a faithful friend
Each foe.

God speed the hour, the glorious hour,
When none on earth
Shall exercise a lordly power,
Nor in a tyrant's presence cower;
But to all manhood's stature tower,
By equal birth!
That hour will come, to each, to all,
And from his prison-house, to thrall
Go forth.

Until that year, day, hour, arrive,
With head, and heart, and hand I'll strive,
To break the rod, and rend the gyve,
The spoiler of his prey deprive—
So witness Heaven!
And never from my chosen post,

Whate'er the peril or the cost,
Be driven.

"

Douglass remained a prominent spokesperson for the abolitionists throughout the 1850s and during the Civil War in the early 1860s. The respect he enjoyed in the North was so great that he even served as an unofficial advisor to Abraham Lincoln. In this role, he urged the president to free all of the slaves. He also led the drive to allow blacks to serve in the Union Army. Outside Washington, Douglass tried to drum up support for the Union with visits to numerous towns and cities. Most of the speeches he gave during this period strongly emphasized his belief that the abolition of slavery was the single most important goal in the Union's conflict with the Confederacy.

After the war ended, Douglass served the federal government in a variety of political and diplomatic positions, including marshal of the District of Columbia and minister to Haiti and the Dominican Republic. He also continued to speak out in his characteristically straightforward fashion. In 1888, for example, he created a national sensation when he gave an angry speech condemning the "so-called emancipation as a stupendous fraud." By the time of his death seven years later, however, the spirit of reform that he had taken such an active role in promoting was only a memory. Once again, African Americans, especially those in the former slave states, found themselves living under conditions similar to those they had known as slaves—or, in some cases, even worse.

Sources

Books

Blassingame, John W., editor, *The Frederick Douglass Papers: Series One—Speeches, Debates, and Interviews,* Volume 1: *1841-46,* 1979, Volume 2: *1847-54,* 1982, Volume 3: *1855-63,* 1985, Volume 4: *1874-80,* 1991, Yale University Press.

Bontemps, Arna, *Free at Last: The Life of Frederick Douglass,* Dodd, Mead, 1971.

Douglass, Frederick, *My Bondage and My Freedom* (reprint), University of Illinois Press, 1987.

Foner, Philip S., editor, *The Voice of Black America: Major Speeches by Negroes in the United States, 1797–1971,* Simon & Schuster, 1972.

Foner, Philip S., *The Life and Writings of Frederick Douglass,* five volumes, International Publishers Company, 1975.

Hill, Roy L., *Rhetoric of Racial Revolt,* Golden Bell Press, 1964.

Huggins, Nathan Irvin, *Slave and Citizen: The Life of Frederick Douglass,* Little, Brown, 1980.

Martin, Waldo E., Jr., *The Mind of Frederick Douglass,* University of North Carolina Press, 1984.

O'Neill, Daniel J., editor, *Speeches by Black Americans,* Dickenson, 1971.

Meltzer, Milton, editor, *The Black Americans: A History in Their Own Words, 1619–1983,* Crowell, 1984.

Smith, Arthur L., *Rhetoric of Black Revolution,* Allyn & Bacon, 1969.

Smith, Arthur L., and Stephen Robb, editors, *The Voice of Black Rhetoric: Selections,* Allyn & Bacon, 1971.

Rita Dove

1952–

Poet

On May 18, 1993, Rita Dove became the first black American woman and the youngest person ever to be named United States poet laureate (see box on page 89). This honor is usually reserved for older, well-established poets who are nearing the end of their careers, but the youthful and energetic Dove brought new life to the position, using the exposure to change the public's perception of poetry.

Early Life

A native of Akron, Ohio, Dove has been composing poetry, plays, and stories since childhood. When she first entered Ohio's Miami University, however, she planned to become a lawyer—until she realized that she really didn't have the talent or the desire to excel in that profession. Instead, she found herself drawn to creative writing. By her junior year she had made up her mind to become a poet.

After graduating from Miami with honors in 1973, Dove studied in Germany for a year. She returned to the United

"THE PREVAILING NOTIONS OUR SOCIETY HARBORS ABOUT THE CREATIVE ARTS MAKES IT DIFFICULT FOR ALL ARTISTS, AND ESPECIALLY THAT LOFTY BREED OF POETS, TO BE TAKEN SERIOUSLY, OR EVEN TO BE TAKEN INTO ACCOUNT."

States to attend the prestigious University of Iowa Writers' Workshop, from which she received her master's degree in creative writing in 1977. Since then, Dove has divided her time between writing, traveling, and teaching.

Dove's goal as a poet has been to take ordinary people or events and, through the magic of verse, show their special beauty and meaning. Her poems are often drawn from her own life or from history and legend. For example, her collection of short poems called Thomas and Beulah, *loosely based on the lives of her maternal grandparents, skillfully combines biography and social history to represent a period of nearly fifty years.*

*Dove is the author of several other volumes of poetry, a book of short stories (*Fifth Sunday*), a novel (*Through the Ivory Gate*), and a verse drama (*The Darker Face of the Earth*). She has been very successful at her craft, earning praise from critics and winning a number of important awards, including the 1987 Pulitzer Prize for* Thomas and Beulah.

Brings Fresh Perspective to Poet Laureate Position

Dove took office as poet laureate only a few months after fellow writer Maya Angelou created and read a special poem to honor the inauguration of President Bill Clinton. The event touched off the public's interest in verse, and Dove decided to take advantage of the situation by scheduling a series of poetry readings at the Library of Congress. Audiences enjoyed the innovative and unusual presentations she organized that combined poetry with other media such as music and photography.

Throughout her two terms as poet laureate, Dove continued to work with the Library of Congress to set up various programs designed to encourage a wider appreciation of poetry. Taking her message beyond Washington, D.C., Dove "visited" classrooms across the nation via interactive video to stimulate interest in poetry among students. She also tried to persuade television executives to air public service announcements consisting of a brief poem and some animation.

On March 17, 1994, Dove shared her thoughts on poetry and the poet laureate position with members of the

Poets Laureate

Poet laureate is a formal title given to poets in Great Britain and the United States. The custom, adopted from the ancient Greek and Roman custom of crowning the poet with a wreath of laurels, dates back to the 1600s in Great Britain, when the king or queen first chose an "official" poet to compose poems in honor of certain special events in the life of the nation and the royal family. Once chosen, the British poet laureate holds the position for the rest of his or her life.

In the United States, the tradition began with a 1985 act by Congress, which eliminated the old title of poetry consultant to the Library of Congress (the national library of the United States) and created the new title of poet laureate consultant. The Librarian of Congress names the poet laureate for a one-year term, but one person may hold the post for a series of terms. Unlike the British poet laureate, the U.S. poet laureate is not required to write any poetry. All he or she must do is give one public poetry reading and deliver one lecture during his or her term. The idea is to give poets laureate as much freedom as possible to work on their own projects.

Most poets laureate do public service in their appointments, however. Some have chosen to meet with students to teach them about poetry and encourage them to write. Others have focused on setting up poetry readings in as many public places as possible. Most have also actively supported the Library's efforts to expand its collection of recorded poetry and literature. In addition, poets laureate usually suggest the names of other writers the Library might want to feature in its literary series and help plan special Library programs.

National Press Club in Washington, D.C. The poet herself furnished a transcription of her remarks.

...As poet laureate I am continually being asked to clarify my position—to list my duties, to elaborate on my plans for promoting the arts. I am usually asked to define poetry as well. Rarely does a journalist ask about poems themselves. In fact, one television reporter confessed afterwards he had been so nervous about our interview that he had **solicited** advice from his colleagues before venturing over to the Poetry Room at the Library of Congress. The **consensus** in his office was: "Ask her how she started writing and who her favorite poets are ... but don't ask her about poems!" So what I want to do today ... is to chase some of the bugaboos about poetry out of this room and, hopefully, from

solicited: asked for.

consensus: a judgment agreed upon by a group of people.

the hearts of those on the receiving end of the radio waves traversing America.

"Poetry—merely whispering its name frightens it away," said [French writer and filmmaker] Jean Cocteau. Today, in our country, we could change that remark to: Poetry—merely whispering its name frightens everyone away.... There are a thousand and one myths about artists in general, and poets in particular: poets are eccentric, poets are not quite of this world; poets are blessed with imagination that the rest of the population can never hope to approach, poets lead wild—or at the very least, wildly disorganized—lives, and enjoy saying outrageous things in polite company. The prevailing notions our society harbors about the creative arts makes it difficult for all artists, and especially that lofty breed of poets, to be taken seriously, or even to be taken into account.

There was a time when I would hide behind less than the whole truth when asked what I "did" in life. As long as I was a student, it was easy: I was an English major, then, a graduate student. After graduation, I satisfied the curiosity of casual acquaintances by timidly saying: I'm working on a book. Later, after I'd begun to teach at a university, I shied away from the easy partial truth of my official designation; although I was an English professor, it sounded **fraudulent** to me, for I had nothing to do with the brilliant second-guessing of dead writers that one associates with English professors, instead I was myself a poet and very much alive, thank you. So I fudged by slurring all my occupations together: I'm a writer and teach creative writing.

Then about twelve years ago, a young woman started up a conversation at a bus stop and posed the inevitable question. I hedged, saying, "I write," to which she replied cheerfully, "Oh, I do calligraphy, too!" That day I made a vow to tell the uncompromised truth. So now when asked what I do for a living, I answer: I'm a poet; I write poetry—and endure one of two reactions caused by my confession: either they grab my sleeve and regale me with the story of great-aunt Maud whose delightful verses brought such joy to family festivities and yet, as hard as she tried, poor soul, could never get her wonderful manuscript published. Then they might look at me as if I, as a published poet, was part of the conspiracy of the modern language mafia who had deprived their great-

fraudulent: misleading, false.

Rita Dove

aunt Maud of her deserved recognition as a master word-smith in the Mother Goose tradition. Or my confession might cause confusion, embarrassment, a kind of bumbling discomfort. The more damaging of the two notions is this one—that poetry is **hermetic,** cerebral stuff, impossible for mere mortals to comprehend.

So where does poetry reside? Where does it begin? When the [French] painter Edgar Degas claimed to be full of ideas for poems, his friend [the French poet Stéphane] Mallarmé said, "My dear Degas, poems are not made out of ideas; they're made out of *words.*" But [American essayist and poet Ralph Waldo] Emerson reminds us: "Words are also actions, and actions are a kind of words." Although it turns upon the action of words, poetry roots in the acts of life. It springs from inner sources that are at the very core of our human-ness—it resides in the **interstices** between the world and the **unarticulated** emotions **circumscribing** our souls.

Instead of sliding deeper into philosophical discourse, I'd like to offer an example from my own work.

My third poetry book, *Thomas and Beulah,* is based on the lives of my maternal grandparents, but it rapidly became an **amalgam** of biographical fact, imagination, and creative scholarship. *Thomas and Beulah* began, though, with a real event—one that was insignificant in the grand context of history but indispensable within the confines of personal biography (an incident time had condensed into an anecdote).

My grandfather died when I was thirteen years old. The family took turns keeping Grandma company; since I wasn't old enough to date, I was the perfect candidate for the week-end slot. One Saturday morning at breakfast, Grandma fixed me the one permitted cup of sweetened coffee, sat down, and related an incident from my grandfather's life before he met her, just as he must have told it to her countless times.

In his late teens, my grandfather worked the Mississippi riverboats as part of a song-and-dance duo. Late one night on the boat, my grandfather dared his mandolin-playing friend to swim across the river to an island where a chestnut tree was growing. The friend dove into the Mississippi and head-ed for the tree—when the island sank and the **maelstrom** sucked him down.

hermetic: obscure, difficult to understand.

interstices: small spaces.

unarticulated: unspoken, not clearly expressed.

circumscribing: surrounding.

amalgam: blend.

maelstrom: whirlpool.

This "true story", as you can see, was pretty unbelievable. Chestnut trees in the middle of the Mississippi—okay. But islands that sink? As my daughter would say: Come on; get real.

My grandmother, however, stuck to her story, with an obstinance that made the anecdote undeniable. Many years later, I recognized it as the crucial point in my grandfather's life—that moment when Fate steps in and your life takes a sickening ninety-degree-turn and plops you down facing the wilderness. We've all had those moments, and the events surrounding it, recalled later, seem surreal, with the slow-motion over-magnification of anything worried over, obsessed over time and time again. Here's the poem:

The Event

Ever since they'd left the Tennessee ridge
with nothing to boast of
but good looks and a mandolin,

the two Negroes leaning
on the rail of a riverboat
were inseparable: Lem plucked

to Thomas's silver falsetto.
But the night was hot and they were drunk.
They spat where the wheel

churned mud and moonlight,
they called to the tarantulas
down among the bananas

to come out and dance.
*You're so fine and mighty; let's see
what you can do,* said Thomas, pointing

to a tree-capped island.
Lem stripped, spoke easy: *Them's chestnuts,
I believe.* Dove

quick as a gasp. Thomas, dry
on deck, saw the green crown shake
as the island slipped
under, dissolved
in the thickening stream.
At his feet,

a stinking circle of rags,
a half-shell mandolin.
Where the wheel turned the water
gently shirred.

Now this story was my own; it haunted me. I wanted to know how to go on after that sickening turn. I asked myself: What are you going to do now, Rita?, and the answer came like an echo: Pick up the mandolin!

I don't know if my grandfather picked up his friend's mandolin or not. (Actually, my mother corrected me when I "interviewed" her for "material" for *Thomas and Beulah*—my grandfather had played the guitar when he was young, not mandolin. I had remembered incorrectly. Or did I? As Stravinsky said: "One lives by memory ... and not by truth.") Well, my Thomas picks up that mandolin and the scraps of his partner's life, and he learns his double-stringed song. He gives up the riverboat life, continues north, and finally settles down in Akron, Ohio, the rubber-baron city built on the banks of the crooked Cuyahoga River, which was then forced underground to service man's factories, man's dreams of industry and wealth. Today that river, rich with chemicals and waste products, has burned more than once, inspiring that Randy Newman song which goes:

Now the Lord can make you tumble
The Lord can make you turn;
The Lord can make you overflow,
But the Lord can't make you burn.

When Thomas lands in Akron in 1921, however, it's still a city "on the up and up," the American Dream in full flower beneath the gritty stench of vulcanized rubber and the ever-present time clock. And there I got stuck. For what did I know about this town in 1921? How could I begin to follow Thomas through those streets if I didn't know what they looked like—how many black people he would see in passing, what a black working-class man could or couldn't do in 1921, what his hopes for the future might have been grounded on?

So I went to the library and amassed notes on working conditions in the factories, census reports, **demographical** charts. I learned how rubber is **vulcanized** and the times of

demographical: relating to the statistical characteristics of the human population.

vulcanized: given strength and elasticity through a chemical process.

the factory shifts; how many white workers from West Virginia were recruited in proportion to black southerners. I learned that the Goodyear Aerospace airdock was, around 1930, the largest structure of its time without interior supports, and that it was so vast, it had its own weather system; occasionally lightning would spark or fog accumulate under the dome.

And how much of this material did I actually use? Next to nothing. The process was very much like interviewing: Ask probing questions, talk to the subject for as long as you can before you get thrown out. And since you've only got a limited space—say 750 words, give or take a few—you look for an angle. I call it the "hinge"—that which swings open the door into the world of that poem—the color of a scarf, or the number of upholstery studs in a leather-backed office chair.

Frustrated, I interrupted my writing long enough to bake some oatmeal cookies—and as usual burned the first tray. That stench stopped me right in my tracks. Because I knew this smell, and not just from other failed batches. I had lived in it. Walked in it.

You see, the Akron where I grew up was governed by two scents: the smell of the rubber factories, and the smell of burning oats from the Quaker Oats silos. They were so prevalent that they had become normal, a part of life. Neither was pleasant, but both aroused the imagination of children. The rubber brought to mind huge truck tires rolling anywhere as long as it was out of Akron; later, in geography class, we dreamed of the massive, **implacable** rubber trees in India whose lashed sides streamed white latex. And the Quaker Oats smell brought a feeling of security, the comfort of the kitchen and its warm oven. It was a delicious push-pull I had forgotten.

So I entered my grandfather's Akron again through smell.

Quaker Oats

The grain elevators have stood empty for years. They used to feed an entire nation of children. Hunched in red leatherette breakfast-nooks, fingers dreaming, children let their spoons clack on the white sides of their bowls. They stare at the carton on the table, a miniature silo with a kindly face smiling under a stiff black hat.

implacable: rigid, unyielding.

They eat their oats with milk and butter and sugar. They eat their oats in their sleep, where horsedrawn carts jolt along miry roads, past cabins where other children wait, half-frozen under tattered counterpanes. The man with the black hat, a burlap sack tucked under his arm, steps down from the wagon whispering *come out, don't be afraid.*

And they come, the sick and the healthy; the red, the brown, the white; the ruddy and the sallow; the curly and the lank. They tumble from rafters and crawl out of trundles. He gives them to eat. He gives them prayers and a good start in the morning. He gives them free enterprise; he gives them the flag and PA systems and roller skates and citizenship. He gives them a tawny canoe to portage overland, through the woods, through the midwestern snow.

The first half of *Thomas and Beulah* is Thomas's story; the second half is determined by his wife. Beulah is a self-taught **milliner** who picked up the skill while working in a dress shop, so she is very aware of color and texture. Thomas's favorite color, blue, becomes the memory trigger in the poem "Wingfoot Lake," becoming the perfect blue of a forbidden, because segregated, swimming pool, and also the blue of redemption, giving equal time to the blue sky of a Fourth of July picnic as well as the blue sky over the heads of the civil rights demonstrators marching through Washington, D.C., on August 28, 1963:

Wingfoot Lake
(Independence Day, 1964)

On her 36th birthday, Thomas had shown her
her first swimming pool. It had been
his favorite color, exactly—just
so much of it, the swimmers' white arms jutting
into the chevrons of high society.
She had rolled up her window
and told him to drive on, fast.

Now this *act of mercy:* four daughters
dragging her to their husbands' company picnic,
white families on one side and them
on the other, unpacking the same
squeeze bottles of Heinz, the same
waxy beef patties and Salem potato chip bags.
So he was dead for the first time
on Fourth of July—ten years ago

had been harder, waiting for something to happen,
and ten years before that, the girls
like young horses eyeing the track.
Last August she stood alone for hours

milliner: a person who makes hats.

in front of the T.V. set
as a crow's wing moved slowly through
the white streets of government.
That brave swimming

scared her, like Joanna saying,
Mother, we're Afro-Americans now!
What did she know about Africa?
Were there lakes like this one
with a rowboat pushed under the pier?
Or Thomas' Great Mississippi
with its sullen silks? (There was
the Nile but the Nile belonged

to God.) Where she came from
was the past, 12 miles into town
where nobody had locked their back door,
and Goodyear hadn't begun to dream of a park
under the company symbol, a white foot
sprouting two small wings.

Although that poem revolves around recognizable historical events, the world arena is **peripheral** to the details of
the picnic. Human beings do not live for history; they may
live under its thrall or in spite of it, even in it—but not
because of history.

Why does poetry affect us differently than, say, a newspaper feature, or a documentary, or even a miniseries? Let me
read to you one woman's reaction, one from what are now
well over a thousand letters I've received since assuming the
poet laureateship. Dinny Moses from Putney, Vermont,
writes:

> I am not a poet, formal or learned. And I certainly don't
> understand it intellectually. However, the musician in me and
> the healer are very drawn to it as a medicine of expression.
> Maybe because it can have a quality of intimacy that I feel
> comfortable with. And in the past three years I find myself at
> times flooding with words that demand to be put to paper,
> unbidden by me consciously. But this outpouring is a kind of
> therapy, I suppose. I call it poetry.

I am always astonished when people claim that poetry is
"intellectual" or "elitist," that it has to do with "books and
flowers and stuff." To me, a poem is so firmly rooted in the

peripheral: outside,
beyond.

world—or rather, the **juncture** between the world and the individual spirit—that I find poems more useful for negotiating the terms of our identities, more **efficacious** in providing a stay against extinction than the mass media. Mass media can provide us with the news but they can't tell us what to do with it. Of course, it is not the task of the news media to crank out solutions; but with no instructions on how to incorporate what's happening close to home or far away—how to locate our private emotions in the public sentiment—we feel helpless and betrayed.

It is a pity that large segments of our society regard the creative arts with some degree of apprehension, even suspicion—that they do not expect the arts, especially the arts created by their contemporaries, to be accessible, nor do they see any reason to incorporate the arts into their everyday or professional lives.

Who's afraid of poetry is not as interesting a question as *why* one is afraid, or maybe just apprehensive. Many of those who profess an aversion to poetry have not read a poem since being forced to memorize "Invictus" in the eighth grade—hardly a fair sampling of the field.

A reason that keeps recurring, in an infinite number of variations is: I don't understand it. Other variations on this theme include: It's not about real life. It's old-fashioned. The language is weird. It's too serious, too hermetic, too self-indulgent. You need a PhD to decipher that stuff. It makes me feel stupid. Well, many of us have suffered a classroom experience where our brave interpretation of a teacher's treasured poem was declared "wrong." Poems, then, became coded texts, something you were supposed to decipher, not enjoy. (And for many of us, unfortunately, that was the end of poetry.)

In one of the most popular poems in the English language, one-fifth of the words cannot be found in Webster's dictionary—cannot be found in any dictionary, in fact, because they are nonsense words. That poem is, of course, the "Jabberwocky" by Lewis Carroll, which begins:

'Twas brillig, and the slithy toves
Did gyre and gimble in the wabe:

juncture: intersection.
efficacious: effective.

All mimsy were the borogoves,
And the mome raths outgrabe.

Precocious seven-year-old Alice's tentative response shows that she is both **befuddled** and intrigued:

"It seems very pretty," she said when she had finished it, "but it's rather hard to understand! Somehow it seems to fill my head with ideas—only I don't exactly know what they are!"

Alice then goes on, in spite of her reservations, to give an accurate **gloss** of the narrative, saying "However, *somebody* killed *something:* that's clear at any rate—" That is exactly what happens in the poem. Alice got that part right. But the part that fills Alice's head with ideas—that, my friends, is poetry.

99

After completing her second term as poet laureate in May 1995, Dove returned to teaching at the University of Virginia in Charlottesville.

Sources

Books

Dictionary of Literary Biography, Volume 120: *American Poets Since World War II,* Gale, 1992.

Dove, Rita, *Thomas and Beulah,* Carnegie-Mellon University Press, 1986.

Dove, Rita, *Grace Notes,* Norton, 1989.

Periodicals

Detroit News, "A 'Poet of Distinction' Assumes Laureate Post," May 19, 1993, p. 5A.

Ebony, "Introducing: Pulitzer Prize-Winning Poet Rita Dove," October 1987, pp. 44-46.

Ms., "Bold Type: Rita Dove, People's Poet," November/December 1993, p. 66.

New York Review of Books, "In the Zoo of the New," October 23, 1986, pp. 47-52.

befuddled: puzzled, confused.

gloss: explanation.

New York Times, "Rita Dove Named Next Poet Laureate; First Black in Post," May 19, 1993; June 20, 1993.

People, "Lovely Meter, Rita-Made: Pulitzer Prize-Winner Rita Dove Puts a New Face on the Poet Laureate's Job," May 31, 1993, p. 92.

Time, "Poetry in Motion," May 31, 1993, p. 73; "Rooms of Their Own," October 18, 1993, pp. 88-89.

Washington Post, April 17, 1987; May 19, 1993.

W. E. B. Du Bois

1868–1963

Educator, writer, and human rights activist

In 1895, **Booker T. Washington** (see entry) gave a landmark speech known as the "Atlanta Compromise." In his remarks, he urged his fellow blacks to set aside their desire for equality and work toward economic advancement instead. The speech drew widespread attention and praise, especially from whites who quickly came to regard Washington as the chief spokesperson for his race. But he did not by any means represent the views of all African Americans. One of his harshest critics was the brilliant scholar William Edward Burghardt (W. E. B.) Du Bois, who insisted that blacks had a right and a duty to demand their political, social, and civil rights as American citizens.

Early Life

Du Bois (pronounced "du boys") was born and raised in Massachusetts. His father deserted the family when Du Bois was just a baby, and his mother, who was partially paralyzed from a stroke, had to struggle to support herself and

"UPON THE FOUNDATION STONE OF A FEW WELL-EQUIPPED NEGRO COLLEGES OF HIGH AND HONEST STANDARDS CAN BE BUILT A PROPER SYSTEM OF FREE COMMON SCHOOLS IN THE SOUTH FOR THE MASSES OF THE NEGRO PEOPLE; ANY ATTEMPT TO FOUND A SYSTEM OF PUBLIC SCHOOLS ON ANYTHING LESS THAN THIS IS ... TO CALL BLIND LEADERS FOR THE BLIND.

her son. Relatives and neighbors helped out as much as they could. Later, when Du Bois himself was old enough to work, he chopped wood, shoveled coal, and did other chores to earn a little money.

*An excellent student, Du Bois was able to attend college thanks to some people in his hometown who recognized his great potential and wanted to make sure he was able to develop it. He received a bachelor's degree from Fisk University in 1888 and earned a second one from Harvard University two years later. He then went on to graduate school in Germany at the University of Berlin. Returning to the United States in 1894, he taught briefly at Ohio's Wilberforce University before joining the faculty of the University of Pennsylvania in Philadelphia. While there he conducted ground-breaking **sociological** research on a local black ghetto. It was the first such study ever to focus on African Americans.*

Develops the Field of Black Sociology

*In 1897, Du Bois became professor of history and economics at Atlanta University in Georgia. During his twelve years there, he established black sociology as a legitimate (accepted or recognized) field of study. He also directed a series of annual conferences on the problems facing black Americans that enhanced his reputation as a scholar and earned him national recognition. This pioneering work often brought him into contact with many other black **intellectuals** who shared his concern about advancing the civil rights of Africans and their descendants throughout the world. These reformers launched the Pan-African movement, which promoted the idea of international unity among all black people to achieve common goals. Du Bois ended up serving as the movement's guiding spirit for virtually the rest of his life.*

In 1903, Du Bois published a collection of essays entitled The Souls of Black Folk *that examined many different social and political issues of importance to blacks. One of its chapters, entitled "On Booker T. Washington and Others," made him the center of a huge controversy. In that particular essay, he argued against Washington's very popular philosophy of **accommodationism.** Du Bois insisted*

sociological: having to do with the study of human society, social institutions, and social relationships.

intellectuals: people who are devoted to the world of ideas and learning.

accommodationism: adapting to the ideas and attitudes of others.

*Du Bois on higher education:
"We need a few strong,
well-equipped Negro colleges,
and we need them now...."*

*that it was foolish and perhaps even dangerous for blacks to remain **submissive** in the belief that whites would eventually "reward" them with equal rights.*

The essay touched off a bitter feud between Washington and Du Bois. Their relationship grew even more tense as Du Bois toured the country delivering his message on the lec-

submissive: yielding to the authority or will of others.

ture circuit. Again and again, he explained how vital it was to the future of black America that its brightest young people (whom he referred to as "the Talented Tenth") receive an education that included more than just training in practical, work-related skills such as carpentry, blacksmithing, sewing, and cooking. This was an obvious jab at Washington and the industrial arts training school he established and headed, Alabama's Tuskegee Institute.

Du Bois's own thoughts on educating African Americans are contained in a speech he gave after the publication of "On Booker T. Washington and Others." Entitled "The Training of Negroes for Social Power," it is excerpted here from Volume 1 of W. E. B. Du Bois Speaks, *edited by Philip S. Foner, Pathfinder Press, 1970.*

"

The responsibility for their own social regeneration ought to be placed largely upon the shoulders of the Negro people. But such responsibility must carry with it a grant of power; responsibility without power is a mockery and a farce. If, therefore, the American people are sincerely anxious that the Negro shall put forth his best efforts to help himself, they must see to it that he is not deprived of the freedom and power to strive....

Such social power means, assuredly, the growth of **initiative** among Negroes, the spread of independent thought, the expanding consciousness of manhood; and these things today are looked upon by many with **apprehension** and distrust.... Men openly declare their **design** to train these millions as a subject **caste,** as men to be thought for, but not to think; to be led, but not to lead themselves.... [But] the American people must come to realize that the responsibility for **dispelling** ignorance and poverty and uprooting crime among Negroes cannot be put upon their own shoulders unless they are given such independent leadership in intelligence, skill, and morality as will inevitably lead to an independent manhood which cannot and will not rest in bonds.

Let me illustrate my meaning particularly in the matter of educating Negro youth.

regeneration: restoration or renewal; improvement.

initiative: the energy and ambition to start up an action

apprehension: fear.

design: intention, plan.

caste: class.

dispelling: eliminating.

W. E. B. Du Bois

The Negro problem, it has often been said, is largely a problem of ignorance—not simply of **illiteracy,** but a deeper ignorance of the world and its ways, of the thought and experience of men; an ignorance of self and the possibilities of human souls. This can be gotten rid of only by training; and primarily such training must take the form of that sort of social leadership which we call education. To apply such leadership to themselves, and to profit by it, means that Negroes would have among themselves men of careful training and broad culture, as teachers and teachers of teachers.... It is, therefore, of crying necessity among Negroes that the heads of their educational system—the teachers in the normal schools, the heads of high schools, the principals of public systems, should be unusually well-trained men.... Such educational leaders should be prepared by long and rigorous courses of study similar to those which the world over have been designed to strengthen the intellectual powers, fortify character, and **facilitate** the transmission from age to age of the stores of the world's knowledge.

Not all men—indeed, not the majority of men, only the exceptional few among American Negroes or among any other people—are adapted to this higher training, as, indeed, only the exceptional few are adapted to higher training in any line; but the significance of such men is not to be measured by their numbers, but rather by the numbers of their pupils and followers who are destined to see the world through their eyes, hear it through their trained ears, and speak to it through the music of their words....

The history of civilization seems to prove that no group or nation which seeks advancement and true development can despise or neglect the power of well-trained minds; and this power of intellectual leadership must be given to the talented tenth among American Negroes before this race can seriously be asked to assume the responsibility of dispelling its own ignorance. Upon the foundation stone of a few well-equipped Negro colleges of high and honest standards can be built a proper system of free common schools in the South for the masses of the Negro people; any attempt to found a system of public schools on anything less than this—on narrow ideals, limited or merely technical training—is to call blind leaders for the blind.

illiteracy: the inability to read and write.

facilitate: encourage, promote.

The very first step toward the settlement of the Negro problem is the spread of intelligence. The first step toward wider intelligence is a free public-school system; and the first and most important step toward a public-school system is the equipment and adequate support of a sufficient number of Negro colleges.... Their chief function is the quickening and training of human intelligence; they can do much in the teaching of morals and manners incidentally, but they cannot and ought not to replace the home as the chief moral teacher; they can teach valuable lessons as to the meaning of work in the world, but they cannot replace technical schools and apprenticeship in actual life, which are the real schools of work. Manual training can and ought to be used in these schools, but as a means and not as an end—to quicken intelligence and self-knowledge and not to teach carpentry; just as arithmetic is used to train minds and not to make skilled accountants....

But spread of intelligence alone will not solve the Negro problem. If this problem is largely a question of ignorance, it is also scarcely less a problem of poverty. If Negroes are to assume the responsibility of raising the standards of living among themselves, the power of intelligent work and leadership toward proper industrial ideals must be placed in their hands....

An industrial school, however, does not merely teach technique. It is also a school—a center of moral influence and of mental discipline. As such it has **peculiar** problems in securing the proper teaching force. It demands broadly trained men: the teacher of carpentry must be more than a carpenter, and the teacher of the domestic arts more than a cook; for such teachers must instruct, not simply in manual **dexterity,** but in mental quickness and moral habits. In other words, they must be teachers as well as **artisans.** It thus happens that college-bred men and men from other higher schools have always been in demand in technical schools.... If the college graduates were today withdrawn from the teaching force of the chief Negro industrial schools, nearly every one of them would have to close its doors. These facts are forgotten by such **advocates** of industrial training as oppose the higher schools....

peculiar: unique.
dexterity: skill.
artisans: craftsmen.
advocates: promoters, supporters.

But intelligence and skill alone will not solve the southern problem of poverty. With these must go that combination of homely habits and virtues which we may loosely call thrift. Something of thrift may be taught in school, more must be taught at home; but both these agencies are helpless when organized economic society denies to workers the just reward of thrift and efficiency. And this has been true of black laborers in the South from the time of slavery down through the scandal of the Freedmen's Bank [established by Congress immediately after the Civil War to help former slaves save and manage money] to the **peonage** and crop-lien system of today. If the southern Negro is shiftless, it is primarily because over large areas a shiftless Negro can get on in the world about as well as an industrious black man.... What is the remedy? Intelligence—not simply the ability to read and write or to sew—but the intelligence of a society **permeated** by that larger division of life and broader tolerance which are fostered by the college and university. Not that all men must be college-bred, but that some men, black and white, must be, to **leaven** the ideals of the lump....

Ignorance and poverty are the vastest of the Negro problems. But to these later years have added a third—the problem of Negro crime.... Of course it is false and silly to represent that white women in the South are in daily danger of black assaulters. On the contrary, white womanhood in the South is absolutely safe in the hands of ninety-five percent of the black men—ten times safer than black womanhood is in the hands of white men. Nevertheless, there is a large and dangerous class of Negro criminals, paupers, and outcasts. The existence and growth of such a class, far from causing surprise, should be recognized as the natural result of that social disease called the Negro problem; nearly every **unto-ward** circumstance known to human experience has united to increase Negro crime: the slavery of the past, the sudden emancipation, the narrowing of economic opportunity, the lawless environment of wide regions, the stifling of natural ambition, the **curtailment** of political privilege, the disregard of the **sanctity** of black men's homes, and above all, a system of treatment for criminals calculated to breed crime far faster than all other available agencies could **repress** it. Such a combination of circumstances is as sure to increase

peonage: the state of being legally obligated to someone to work off debts.

permeated: spread throughout.

leaven: raise (in the sense that yeast—a leavening agent—makes a lump of bread dough rise).

untoward: unhappy, unfortunate.

curtailment: reduction.

sanctity: the state of being safe from assault or invasion by others.

repress: control.

the numbers of the vicious and outcast as the rain is to wet the earth. The phenomenon calls for no delicately drawn theories of race differences; it is a plain case of cause and effect.

But, plain as the causes may be, the results are just as **deplorable,** and repeatedly today the criticism is made that Negroes do not recognize sufficiently their responsibility in this matter. Such critics forget how little power today Negroes have over their own lower classes. Before the black murderer who strikes his victim today, the average black man stands far more helpless than the average white, and, too, suffers ten times more from the effects of the deed. The white man has political power, accumulated wealth, and knowledge of social forces; the black man is practically **disfranchised,** poor, and unable to discriminate between the criminal and martyr.... If social reform among Negroes be without organization or trained leadership from within, if the administration of law is always for the avenging of the white victim and seldom for the reformation of the black criminal, if ignorant black men misunderstand the functions of government because they have had no decent instruction, and intelligent black men are denied a voice in government because they are black—under such circumstances to hold Negroes responsible for the suppression of crime among themselves is the cruelest of mockeries.

On the other hand, a sincere desire among the American people to help the Negroes undertake their own social regeneration means, first, that the Negro be given the ballot on the same terms as other men, to protect him against injustice and to safeguard his interests in the administration of law; secondly, that through education and social organization he be trained to work, and save, and earn a decent living. But these are not all; wealth is not the only thing worth accumulating; experience and knowledge can be accumulated and handed down, and no people can be truly rich without them....

Philanthropy and purpose among blacks as well as among whites must be guided and curbed by knowledge and mental discipline—knowledge of the forces of civilization that make for survival, ability to organize and guide those forces, and realization of the true meaning of those broader ideals of

deplorable: disgraceful, shameful.

disfranchised: denied the right to vote.

philanthropy: the donation of money or other kinds of support for humanitarian efforts.

W. E. B. Du Bois

human betterment which may in time bring heaven and earth a little nearer. This is social power—it is gotten in many ways—by experience, by social contact, by what we loosely call the chances of life. But the systematic method of acquiring and **imparting** it is by the training of the youth to thought, power, and knowledge in the school and college....

Three things American slavery gave the Negro—the habit of work, the English language, and the Christian religion; but one priceless thing it **debauched,** destroyed, and took from him, and that was the organized home. For the sake of intelligence and thrift, for the sake of work and morality, this home life must be restored and regenerated with newer ideals. How? The normal method would be by actual contact with a higher home life among his neighbors, but this method the social separation of white and black **precludes.** A proposed method is by schools of domestic arts, but, valuable as these are, they are but **subsidiary** aids to the establishment of homes; for real homes are primarily centers of ideals and teaching and only incidentally centers of cooking. The restoration and raising of home ideals must, then, come from social life among Negroes themselves; and does that social life need no leadership? It needs the best possible leadership of pure hearts and trained heads, the highest leadership of carefully trained men.

Such are the arguments for the Negro college.... We believe that a rationally arranged college course of study for men and women able to pursue it is the best and only method of putting into the world Negroes with ability to use the social forces of their race so as to stamp out crime, strengthen the home, eliminate **degenerates,** and inspire and encourage the higher tendencies of the race not only in thought and aspiration, but in everyday **toil.** And we believe this, not simply because we have argued that such training ought to have these effects, or merely because we hoped for such results in some dim future, but because already for years we have seen in the work of our graduates precisely such results as I have mentioned: successful teachers of teachers, intelligent and upright ministers, skilled physicians, principals of industrial schools, businessmen, and, above all, makers of model homes and leaders of social groups, out from which radiate **subtle** but **tangible** forces of uplift and inspiration.

imparting: sharing, passing something on.

debauched: corrupted.

precludes: prevents, hinders.

subsidiary: secondary, minor.

degenerates: people of low moral character.

toil: work.

subtle: hidden, obscured.

tangible: able to be perceived with the senses; real.

The proof of this lies scattered in every state of the South, and, above all, in the half-unwilling testimony of men **disposed** to **decry** our work.

Between the Negro college and industrial school there are the strongest grounds for cooperation and unity.... We need a few strong, well-equipped Negro colleges, and we need them now, not tomorrow; unless we can have them and have them decently supported, Negro education in the South ... is doomed to failure, and the forces of social regeneration will be fatally weakened, for the college today among Negroes is, just as truly as it was yesterday among whites, the beginning and not the end of human training, the foundation and not the **capstone** of popular education.

Strange, is it not, my brothers, how often in America those great watchwords of human energy—"Be strong!" "Know thyself!" "Hitch your wagon to a star!"—how often these die away into dim whispers when we face these seething millions of black men? And yet do they not belong to them? Are they not their heritage as well as yours? Can they bear burdens without strength, know without learning, and aspire without ideals? Are you afraid to let them try? Fear rather, in this our common fatherland, lest we live to lose those great watchwords of liberty and opportunity which yonder in the eternal hills their fathers fought with your fathers to preserve.

"

*In 1905, Du Bois was one of about thirty blacks whose strong opposition to Booker T. Washington led to the founding of the Niagara Movement. Its members, including anti-lynching activist **Ida B. Wells-Barnett** (see entry), were committed to securing what Du Bois described as "every single right that belongs to a freeborn American, political, civil and social."*

The Niagara Movement fell apart after only a couple of years, however, partly as a result of Washington's attempts to crush it, and partly because its members drifted away to join other civil rights organizations. One of these was the National Association for the Advancement of Colored People (NAACP), which Du Bois also helped establish. He main-

disposed: inclined.

decry: criticize, condemn.

capstone: the topmost stone of a wall, in this sense the high point or crowning achievement.

The Great Depression

From 1929 until about 1940, the United States and much of the rest of the world experienced a period of severe economic crisis known as the Great Depression, or simply the Depression. It was marked by high unemployment, bank failures, factories and other businesses shrinking or shutting down completely, and families losing their savings, their farms, and their homes. This downturn hit blacks especially hard; as some of them bitterly observed, they were "the last hired and the first fired."

Discrimination also played a part in preventing blacks from taking full advantage of the various federal relief programs that were established during the 1930s to help those in need. Although the programs originated in Washington, D.C., on orders from the president or Congress, most of them were actually run at the state and local levels by all-white groups of officials. Thus, African Americans often found it difficult to obtain any kind of aid, particularly in the South.

tained an on-again, off-again relationship with the group for nearly forty years, including a long period as editor of its official publication, the Crisis. But Du Bois and his fellow NAACP members often clashed over the group's goals and how they planned to reach them.

One of their major areas of disagreement involved **integration** and **black nationalism.** During the late 1910s and 1920s, Du Bois (like the NAACP) was an outspoken opponent of **Marcus Garvey** (see entry) and the black separatist movement. While he supported the idea of promoting unity among blacks all over the world, he was a firm believer in integration and urged African Americans to keep up the fight for their rights at home.

During the 1930s, however, Du Bois reconsidered his position as he watched blacks suffer tremendously from the effects of the Great Depression. Instead of integration, he began advocating what he called "voluntary segregation"—blacks banding together in their own organizations to help each other. Only then, he said, would they be free of dependence on or interference from whites. (Some thirty years later, the Black Power movement adopted this idea as part of its philosophy.) His position put him at odds with the NAACP, which condemned segregation in any form. In June 1934, the tension between Du Bois and the rest of the

integration: a belief in bringing social groups together by making all institutions and organizations open to all races and ethnic groups without restriction

black nationalism: a belief that blacks should separate from whites and form their own self-governing communities and businesses.

NAACP led him to leave the group. His call for establishing "a Negro nation within the nation" then became a major theme of his speeches.

During the 1950s, Du Bois became the target of police and FBI harassment because of his outspoken admiration for the Soviet Union and **communism.** *Convinced that black Americans would never enjoy freedom in their native land, he left the United States in 1961 to settle in the African nation of Ghana. He died there on August 27, 1963.*

Sources

Books

Du Bois, W. E. B., *In Battle for Peace: The Story of My 83rd Birthday* (reprint), Kraus Reprint, 1976.

Du Bois, W. E. B., *The Autobiography of W.E.B. Du Bois* (reprint), Kraus Reprint, 1976.

Du Bois, W. E. B., *The Souls of Black Folk: Essays and Sketches* (reprint), Random House, 1990.

Duffy, Bernard K., and Halford R. Ryan, editors, *American Orators of the Twentieth Century: Critical Studies and Sources,* Greenwood Press, 1987.

Foner, Philip S., editor, *W. E. B. Du Bois Speaks,* Volume 1: *Speeches and Addresses, 1890–1919,* Volume 2: *Speeches and Addresses, 1920–1963,* Pathfinder Press, 1970.

Hamilton, Virginia, *W. E. B. Du Bois: A Biography,* Crowell, 1972.

Lewis, David, *W. E. B. Du Bois: Biography of a Race, 1868–1919,* Holt, 1993.

Smith, Arthur L., *Rhetoric of Black Revolution,* Allyn & Bacon, 1969.

Stafford, Mark, *W. E. B. Du Bois,* Chelsea House, 1989.

Periodicals

Ebony, "Ten Greats of Black History," August 1972, pp. 35–42.

communism: an economic system in which the government (rather than private individuals or companies) owns and controls the means of producing goods, which are then supposed to be shared by everyone equally.

Marian Wright Edelman

1939–

Lawyer and children's rights activist

Marian Wright Edelman is founding president of the Children's Defense Fund (CDF), a research and lobbying group based in Washington, D.C. (A lobbying group works to try to influence lawmakers about a particular cause.) As head of the CDF, Edelman has become famous throughout the country as an outspoken advocate for children. Her crusade embraces the young of all races and economic backgrounds. But Edelman is especially concerned about those children who spend their lives in a struggle against poverty, racism, violence, substandard education and health care, unemployment, and the many other evils that plague modern society. Her goal is to make sure that every American child enjoys "a healthy start, a head start and a fair start" in life.

Early Life

The daughter of a Baptist preacher, Edelman grew up as part of a loving and secure family in a small South Carolina town. Thanks to her family as well as her teachers and

"IT TAKES JUST ONE PERSON TO CHANGE A CHILD'S LIFE...."

other members of the local black community, she developed a strong sense of self-respect and self-confidence—qualities that helped her cope with the racial injustice she experienced as an African American in the segregated South.

Edelman left her hometown in 1956 to attend Spelman College in Atlanta, Georgia. There she took classes to help her prepare for a career in the foreign service, the branch of the U.S. State Department that includes ambassadors, consuls, and other official government representatives who serve overseas. But her plans soon changed when she became involved in the civil rights movement, which was just beginning to rise up against white racism in the South. Determined to help in the struggle, Edelman decided to go to law school after receiving her bachelor's degree in 1960.

Works for the Civil Rights Movement in Mississippi

Upon her graduation from Yale University three years later, Edelman joined the staff of the National Association for the Advancement of Colored People (NAACP) Legal Defense and Educational Fund. She was then sent to Mississippi, where she became the first black woman admitted to the bar (officially allowed to practice law) in that state. In the beginning, she spent much of her time working on behalf of white student demonstrators from the North who had been jailed for trying to register black voters. Later, she turned her attention to other issues such as improving the economic situation for blacks in Mississippi.

During the course of her work in the civil rights movement, Edelman met many desperately poor children whose difficult lives touched her deeply. Before long, she had made up her mind to try to do something about the extreme poverty that existed in Mississippi and elsewhere in the country. So she headed to Washington, D.C., where she hoped to focus more national attention on the problem.

Establishes the Children's Defense Fund

In 1968, Edelman launched what was known as the Washington Research Project. It was an organization devoted to making the laws and programs already in place work better for the poor. From these efforts sprang the Children's Defense Fund, which Edelman founded in 1973 and still heads. Its aim is to provide a voice for the group she considers the true "silent majority" in America—children (especially poor, minority, and handicapped children) who cannot vote or speak up for themselves. To that end, she lobbies tirelessly in Washington and throughout the country to make sure the needs of the country's youngest citizens are taken into account when legislators create public policy.

Under Edelman's leadership, the CDF has become known nationwide for its strong commitment to improving the lives of children and their families. It has investigated and reported on a wide variety of issues, including health care, teenage pregnancy, education, the juvenile justice system, homelessness, substance abuse, and violence.

Edelman herself keeps in close contact with members of the U.S. Congress to help draft new legislation or to make sure they know the CDF's opinion on bills that have a direct impact on children. She also contributes regularly to magazines and newspapers, grants frequent interviews, and fulfills numerous speaking engagements during the course of a typical year. Her goal is to get the message out to as many people as possible that America's children face an increasingly bleak future unless steps are taken now to reverse years of public indifference to their plight.

On June 9, 1994, Edelman spoke at the graduation ceremonies for Harvard University Medical School. In her talk, she focused on one of the most urgent problems of the 1990s—violence and its effect on children. With a passion for her subject that often leaves her listeners in tears, Edelman condemned the "total breakdown in American values, common sense, and parent and community responsibility to protect and nurture children." She urged all adults to "change ourselves, our hearts, our personal priorities, and our neglect of any of God's children ... to see that no child is left behind." The Children's Defense Fund furnished a copy of her speech, part of which is reprinted here.

“

**Violence romps through our children's play-
grounds,** invades their bedroom slumber parties, terrorizes
their Head Start centers and schools, frolics down the streets
they walk to and from school, dances through their school
buses, waits at the stop light and bus stop, lurks at McDonald's, runs them down on the corner, shoots through their
bedroom windows, attacks their front porches and neighborhoods, strikes them or their parents at home, and tantalizes
them across the television screen every six minutes. It snatch-
es away their family members at work, and at random saps
their energy and will to learn, and makes them forget about
tomorrow. It nags and picks at their minds and spirits day in
and day out, snuffing out the promise and joy of childhood
and of the future which becomes just surviving today.

Inner-city children as young as 10, psychiatrists and social
workers report, think about death all the time and even plan
their own funerals. Young Black and Brown men speak long-
ingly of reaching the ripe old age of 20 in their bullet-rav-
aged, job-destitute, politically forsaken neighborhoods. Some
speak wistfully of prison with "three hots and a cot" as a
safer haven than their dead-end streets and empty, jobless
futures in a society that has decreed them expendable. Dr.
James Garbarino, president of the Erikson Institute, says
American inner-city children are exposed to such heavy
doses of extreme violence they exhibit symptoms of **post-
traumatic stress disorder** like children in war-torn countries such as Mozambique, Cambodia, and Palestine.

At least 13 children die daily from guns, at least 30 other
children are injured every day, adding billions to our out-of-
control public health costs. The National Association of Children's Hospitals and Rehabilitation puts the average child
gun injury hospitalization cost at $14,434.

Although the threat of violence hovers most heavily over
inner cities, it respects no boundaries as the madmen shootings on the Long Island commuter train, downtown San
Francisco office building, and Waco tragedy attest. Violence
was the top worry of parents and children, according to a
1993 *Newsweek*-CDF poll of 10- to 17-year-olds and their parents.

**post-traumatic stress
disorder:** depression,
nervousness, or other
psychological condition
brought on by an extremely
upsetting event.

| Marian Wright Edelman

What Do We Do?

First, recognize that we face a total breakdown in American values, common sense, and parent and community responsibility to protect and nurture children.

Never has America permitted children to rely on guns and gangs rather than parents and neighbors for protection and love or pushed so many children onto the tumultuous sea of life without the life vests of nurturing families and communities, challenged minds, job prospects, and hope.

Never have we exposed children so early and relentlessly to cultural messages glamorizing violence, sex, possessions, alcohol, and tobacco with so few **mediating** influences from responsible adults. And never have we experienced such a numbing and reckless reliance on violence to resolve problems, feel powerful, or be entertained. A single trip to the movies often results in the witnessing of multiple deaths on a scale that makes them seem irrelevant. *New York Times* movie critic Vincent Canby counted 74 dead in *Total Recall,* 81 in *Robocop 2,* 106 in *Rambo III,* and 264 in *Die Hard II.* It's time to say enough. While I am sick of record companies profiting from the violent rap they find a ready market for among white suburban and inner-city youths alike, I am just as sick of *Rambos* and *Terminators,* and of video games like "Mortal Kombat" and "Night Trap" that portray decapitation, murder, and violence as fun and entertainment.

The average preschool child watches over eight-and-one-half months of television before entering school. The lines between make believe and real life blur in **rudderless** child lives unpeopled by enough caring adults transmitting positive values or helping them interpret what they see....

Second, let's stop the adult hypocrisy and double standards. Today, two out of every three Black and one fifth of all White babies are born to never-married mothers. And if it's wrong for 13-year-old inner-city girls to have babies without the benefit of marriage, it's wrong for rich celebrities and we ought to stop putting them on the cover of *People* magazine. It is adults who have engaged in epidemic abuse of children and of each other in our homes. It is adults who have taught children to kill and disrespect human life. It is adults who manufacture, market, and profit from the guns that have

mediating: intervening, moderating.

rudderless: without direction or guidance.

turned many neighborhoods and schools into war zones. It is adults who have financed, produced, directed, and starred in the movies, television shows, and music that have made graphic violence **ubiquitous** in our culture. It is adults who have borne children and then left millions of them behind without basic health care, quality child care and education, or moral guidance. It is adults who have taught our children to look for meaning outside rather than inside themselves, teaching them in Dr. [Martin Luther] King's words "to judge success by the index of our salaries or the size of our automobiles, rather than by the quality of our service and relationship to humanity." And it is adults who have to stand up and be adults and accept our responsibility to parent and protect the young.

Step three is to mount a massive moral witness and **mobilization** against the violence of guns, poverty, and child neglect in American life. The NRA [National Rifle Association], powerful firearms and ammunition manufacturers and sellers, the military-industrial complex, wealthy corporations and individuals who gained most from the unjust economic priorities of the past 12 years, and their political allies, will not untie the noose from our children's necks and nation's future unless a massive movement swells up from every nook and cranny of America. Parent by parent, youth by youth, doctor by doctor, religious congregation by congregation, school by school, and neighborhood by neighborhood, we'll breathe life and security again into our democracy if we are willing to risk our comfort and status today for our children's and nation's tomorrow.

We must begin by taking guns out of the hands of children and those who kill children. Whether you are a hunter, NRA member, gun owner, or not, I hope you will agree that child gun deaths must stop and join in calling for a cease fire and responsible regulation of guns as the dangerous products they are. And I hope you will help spread the message that guns endanger rather than protect. A *New England Journal of Medicine* study found that a handgun in the home is 43 times more likely to be used to kill a family member or friend than for justifiable homicide. Suicide victims are two and a half times more likely to have guns at home. Over half of youth and child suicides involved guns.

ubiquitous: widespread.

mobilization: an effort to bring people together in an orderly and effective way.

Marian Wright Edelman

But crucial gun control is not enough alone to prevent violence and reestablish peace, love and mutual respect in our homes, neighborhoods and society. We must also address the breakdown of spiritual, family, and community norms and just opportunity in America. Whether the focus is on random shootings or the drug epidemic or too early and out-of-wedlock childbearing, we are drawn back to the limited opportunities that lead too many children and adolescents to conclude that they have nothing to gain and little to lose. When our young lack a **stake** in our dominant values and norms, both we and they face a perilous road ahead.

Finally, determine that you will never become **cynical** or despondent about your capacity to help transform America and build nurturing families and caring communities.

Let me end with a story by Elizabeth Ballard about one school teacher, Jean Thompson, and one boy, Teddy Stollard.

On the first day of school, Jean Thompson told her students, "Boys and girls, I love you all the same." Teachers sometimes lie. Little Teddy Stollard was a boy Jean Thompson did not like. He slouched in his chair, didn't pay attention, his mouth hung open in a stupor, his clothes were mussed, his hair unkempt, and he smelled. He was an unattractive boy and Jean Thompson didn't like him.

Teachers have records. And Jean Thompson had Teddy's.

"First grade: Teddy's a good boy. He shows promise in his work and attitude. But he has a poor home situation.

Second grade: Teddy is a good boy. He does what he is told. But he is too serious. His mother is terminally ill.

Third grade: Teddy is falling behind in his work; he needs help. His mother died this year. His father shows no interest.

Fourth grade: Teddy is in deep waters; he is in need of psychiatric help. He is totally withdrawn."

Christmas came, and the boys and girls brought their presents and piled them on her desk. They were all in brightly colored paper except for Teddy's. His was wrapped in brown paper and held together with scotch tape. And on it, scribbled in crayon, were the words, "For Miss Thompson from Teddy." She tore open the brown paper and out fell a rhinestone bracelet with most of the stones missing and a bottle of cheap perfume that was almost empty. When the other boys and girls began to giggle she had enough sense to put some of the perfume on her wrist, put on the bracelet, hold her wrist up to the other children and say, "Doesn't it smell lovely? Isn't the bracelet pretty?" And taking their cue from the teacher, they all agreed.

stake: interest in.
cynical: deeply distrustful.

Marian Wright Edelman

At the end of the day, when all the children had left, Teddy lingered, came over to her desk and said, "Miss Thompson, all day long, you smelled just like my mother. And her bracelet, that's her bracelet, it looks real nice on you too. I'm really glad you like my presents." And when he left, she got down on her knees and buried her head in the chair and she begged God to forgive her.

The next day when the children came, she was a different teacher. She was a teacher with a heart. And she cared for all the children, but especially those who needed help. Especially Teddy. She tutored him and put herself out for him.

By the end of that year, Teddy had caught up with a lot of the children and was even ahead of some.

Several years later, Jean Thompson got this note:

Dear Miss Thompson:

I'm graduating from high school. I wanted you to be the first to know. Love, Teddy.

Four years later she got another note:

Dear Miss Thompson:

I wanted you to be the first to know. The university has not been easy, but I liked it. Love, Teddy Stollard.

Four years later there was another note:

Dear Miss Thompson:

As of today, I am Theodore J. Stollard, M.D. How about that? I wanted you to be the first to know. I'm going to be married in July.... I want you to come and sit where my mother would have sat, because you're the only family I have. Dad died last year.

And she went and she sat where his mother should have sat because she deserved to be there. She had become a decent and loving human being.

There are millions of Teddy Stollards all over our nation— children we have forgotten, given up on, left behind. How many Teddys will never become doctors, lawyers, teachers, police officers, or engineers because there was no Jean Thompson? No you? How many children will never learn enough now to earn a living later because you and I did not reach out to them, speak up for them, vote, lobby, and struggle for them?

How many times will you plead no time when a child seeks your attention, or refuse to serve the poor child because of the paperwork burden, or write off the unruly and unresponsive child in your classroom, agency, or neighborhood because you don't want to expend the energy or simply decide it isn't your job or responsibility?

Any one of us can become a Jean Thompson and every one of us must if we are to feel and heal our children's pain and nation's divisions. It takes just one person to change a child's life and to ensure that children like Teddy are not left behind, have a safe haven from the street, a voice at the end of the phone, time with an attentive Big Sister, Brother, or mentor.

The most important step each of us can take to end the violence and poverty and child neglect that is tearing our country apart is to change ourselves, our hearts, our personal priorities, and our neglect of any of God's children, and add our voice to those of others in a new movement that is bigger than our individual efforts to see that no child is left behind.

Do not be overwhelmed or give up because problems seem so hard or **intractable.** Abraham Lincoln kept going through depression and war and never gave up. And so the American Union was preserved. Martin Luther King, Jr., did not give up when he was scared and depressed and tired and didn't know what next step to take. And so the walls of racial segregation crumbled from his labors and that of countless unsung Black and Brown and White citizens. [The late AIDS activist] Elizabeth Glaser hasn't stopped fighting despite being affected by AIDS for 13 years and the loss of a child to AIDS. Her **dogged** and urgent persistence has contributed to greater attention to this killer disease. [Gun-control activists] Sarah and Jim Brady refused to give up despite setback after setback and opposition from the powerful NRA [National Rifle Association], and the Brady Bill was signed into law in 1993. Millions of children are still beating the odds every day and are staying in school and becoming law-abiding citizens despite the violence and poverty and drugs and family decay all around them. And so you and I can keep on keeping on

intractable: not easily solved.

dogged: determined.

Marian Wright Edelman

until we change the odds for all American children by making the violence of guns, poverty, preventable disease, and family neglect unAmerican.

God speed.

99

On June 1, 1996, more than 200,000 people gathered at the Lincoln Memorial in Washington, D.C., for a "Stand for Children" march and rally organized by the CDF. Edelman had called for the demonstration to fight against what she described as the "evil" attempts in Congress to slash programs that help children, especially poor children. She explained in the New York Times several months earlier, "It's time for mothers ... and fathers ... and grandmothers and grandfathers and nurturers and caregivers and religious leaders to come and say to these people in power in an election year that hurting children is morally and politically unacceptable."

Sources

Books

Edelman, Marian Wright, *Families in Peril: An Agenda for Social Change* (W. E. B. Du Bois Lectures), Harvard University Press, 1987.

Edelman, Marian Wright, *The Measure of Our Success: A Letter to My Children and Yours,* Beacon Press, 1992.

Peterson, Owen, editor, *Representative American Speeches, 1987–1988,* Wilson, 1988.

Periodicals

Ebony, "We Must Not Lose What We Knew Was Right Then," November 1995.

Harper's Bazaar, "Saint Marian," February 1993.

Mother Jones, "Kids First!" May/June 1991.

Ms., "Marian Wright Edelman," July/August 1987.

Newsweek, "A Mother's Guiding Message," June 8, 1992, p. 27; "She's Taking Her Stand," June 10, 1996, p.32.

New Yorker, "A Sense of Urgency," March 27, 1989; "Children of a Lesser Country," January 15, 1996, p. 26.

New York Times, October 8, 1992.

New York Times Book Review, August 23, 1992.

People, "Save the Children," July 6, 1992, pp. 101-102.

Rolling Stone, "Marian Wright Edelman: On the Front Lines of the Battle to Save America's Children," December 10, 1992.

Time, "They Cannot Fend for Themselves," March 23, 1987, p. 27.

Henry Highland Garnet

1815–1882

Clergyman and abolitionist

Among the many prominent figures in the antislavery movement during the mid-nineteenth century, Henry Highland Garnet ranks as one of the most militantly outspoken. His speeches on the subject of slavery are some of the most emotional ever delivered. So radical was Garnet that even many of his fellow black abolitionists (people in favor of getting rid of, or abolishing, slavery) were afraid that his extremism could hurt their cause.

Early Life

Garnet was the son of a slave woman and an African chief who had been kidnapped and sold into bondage. He was only nine years old when his family escaped from a Maryland plantation and settled in New York City. Young Henry then enrolled in a private school maintained by the black community. There his public speaking ability first attracted attention.

In 1835 Garnet headed north to continue his studies at the Canaan Academy in Canaan, New Hampshire. But

"YOU HAD FAR BETTER ALL DIE—DIE IMMEDIATELY, THAN LIVE SLAVES, AND ENTAIL YOUR WRETCHEDNESS UPON YOUR POSTERITY."

when he arrived on campus, an angry mob opposed to the education of blacks burned down the school rather than see its doors opened to him. He then went back to New York to prepare for a career in the ministry and graduated in 1840 from the Oneida Institute in Whitestown. Garnet then served as a pastor for a number of different congregations in the state of New York and throughout various island nations of the West Indies before accepting a position at New York City's Shiloh Presbyterian Church. He remained there for more than forty years.

At Shiloh, Garnet's fiery antislavery sermons soon made him the best-known black clergyman in the city. He branded white Southerners as devils. He blasted white Northerners for quietly going about their lives as if the evils of slavery did not exist. And he repeatedly urged slaves to revolt against their masters, no matter what the consequences.

Urges Slaves to Revolt

*On August 22, 1843, Garnet delivered his most warlike call-to-arms to enslaved blacks in the South. The occasion was a meeting of free black men in Buffalo, New York, known as the National Convention of Colored Citizens. Among those in attendance were such up-and-coming public figures as **Frederick Douglass** (see entry) and William Wells Brown. But Garnet's extremism alarmed this group of rather moderate abolitionists. In fact, his "Address to the Slaves of the United States of America" was so controversial that delegates voted against publishing and distributing it as an official document of the convention.*

Five years later, in 1848, Garnet himself finally had copies of his "Address" printed. He bound it with David Walker's famous Appeal, *an equally inflammatory piece that had first appeared in 1829. Garnet's speech was later reprinted in* The Voice of Black Rhetoric: Selections, *edited by Arthur L. Smith and Stephen Robb, Allyn & Bacon, 1971. It is from that book that the following version was taken.*

Address to the Slaves of the United States of America

Brethren and fellow citizens: Your brethren of the North, East, and West have been accustomed to meet together in national conventions, to sympathize with each other, and to weep over your unhappy condition. In these meetings we have addressed all classes of the free, but we have never, until this time, sent a word of consolation and advice to you. We have been contented in sitting still and mourning over your sorrows, earnestly hoping that before this day your sacred liberties would have been restored. But, we have hoped in vain. Years have rolled on, and tens of thousands have been borne on streams of blood and tears to the shores of eternity. While you have been oppressed, we have also been partakers with you; nor can we be free while you are enslaved. We, therefore, write to you as being bound with you....

Slavery has fixed a deep gulf between you and us, and while it shuts out from you the relief and consolation which your friends would willingly render, it afflicts and persecutes you with a fierceness which we might not expect to see in the fiends of hell. But still the Almighty Father of mercies has left to us a glimmering ray of hope, which shines out like a lone star in a cloudy sky. Mankind are becoming wiser, and better—the oppressor's power is fading, and you, every day, are becoming better informed, and more numerous. Your **grievances,** brethren, are many. We shall not attempt, in this short address, to present to the world all the dark catalogue of the nation's sins, which have been committed upon an innocent people. Nor is it indeed necessary, for you feel them from day to day, and all the civilized world looks upon them with amazement.

Two hundred and twenty-seven years ago the first of our injured race were brought to the shores of America. They came not with their own consent, to find an unmolested enjoyment of the blessings of this fruitful soil. The first dealings they had with men calling themselves Christians exhibited to them the worst features of corrupt and sordid hearts: and convinced them that no cruelty is too great, no villainy and no robbery too **abhorrent** for even enlightened men to perform, when influenced by **avarice** and lust. Neither did they come flying upon the wings of Liberty to a land of freedom. But they came with broken hearts, from their beloved native land, and were doomed to **unrequited** toil and deep

grievances: complaints.

abhorrent: hateful, horrible.

avarice: greed, selfishness.

unrequited: unrewarded.

degradation. Nor did the evil of their bondage end at their emancipation by death. Succeeding generations inherited their chains, and millions have come from eternity into time, and have returned again to the world of spirits, cursed and ruined by American slavery.

The **propagators** of the system, or their immediate successors, very soon discovered its growing evil, and its tremendous wickedness, and secret promises were made to destroy it. The gross inconsistency of a people holding slaves, who had themselves "ferried o'er the wave" for freedom's sake, was too apparent to be entirely overlooked. The voice of Freedom cried, "Emancipate your slaves." Humanity **supplicated** with tears for the deliverance of the children of Africa. Wisdom urged her solemn plea. The bleeding captive plead [sic] his innocence, and pointed to Christianity who stood weeping at the cross. Jehovah frowned upon the **nefarious** institution, and thunderbolts, red with vengeance, struggled to leap forth to blast the guilty wretches who maintained it. But all was vain. Slavery had stretched its dark wings of death over the land, the Church stood silently by—the priests prophesied falsely, and the people loved to have it so. Its throne is established, and now it reigns triumphant.

Nearly three millions of your fellow citizens are prohibited by law and public opinion (which in this country is stronger than law) from reading the Book of Life. Your intellect has been destroyed as much as possible, and every ray of light they have attempted to shut out from your minds. The oppressors themselves have become involved in the ruin. They have become weak, sensual, and **rapacious**—they have cursed you—they have cursed themselves—they have cursed the earth which they have trod.

The colonies threw the blame upon England. They said that the mother country **entailed** the evil upon them, and they would rid themselves of it if they could. The world thought they were sincere, and the **philanthropic** pitied them. But time soon tested their sincerity. In a few years the colonists grew strong, and severed themselves from the British government. Their independence was declared, and they took their station among the sovereign powers of the earth. The declaration was a glorious document. Sages admired it, and the patriotic of every nation reverenced the Godlike sentiments which

propagators: those who extend or increase something.

supplicated: begged.

nefarious: evil, criminal.

rapacious: grasping, greedy.

entailed: imposed, forced.

philanthropic: charitable, generous with money or other kinds of support for humanitarian efforts.

Henry Highland Garnet

it contained. When the power of government returned to their hands, did they emancipate the slaves? No; they rather added new links to our chains. Were they ignorant of the principles of liberty? Certainly they were not. The sentiments of their revolutionary orators fell in burning eloquence upon their hearts, and with one voice they cried, liberty or death. Oh, what a sentence was that! It ran from soul to soul like electric fire, and nerved the arms of thousands to fight in the holy cause of freedom....

Slavery! How much misery is comprehended in that single word. What mind is there that does not shrink from its direful effects? Unless the image of God be obliterated from the soul, all men cherish the love of

Africans disembark from slave ships on American shores: "They came with broken hearts, from their beloved native lands, and were doomed to unrequited toil and deep degradation."—Henry Highland Garnet

liberty. The nice discerning political economist does not regard the sacred right more than the untutored African who roams in the wilds of Congo. Nor has the one more right to the full enjoyment of his freedom than the other. In every man's mind the good seeds of liberty are planted, and he who brings his fellow down so low, as to make him contented with a condition of slavery, commits the highest crime against God and man. Brethren, your oppressors aim to do this. They endeavor to make you as much like brutes as possible. When they have blinded the eyes of your mind—when they have embittered the sweet waters of life—when they have shut out the light which shines from the word of God—then, and not till then, has American slavery done its perfect work.

TO SUCH DEGRADATION IT IS SINFUL IN THE EXTREME FOR YOU TO MAKE VOLUNTARY SUBMISSION. The divine commandments you are in duty bound to reverence and obey. If you do not obey them, you will surely meet with the displeasure of the Almighty. He requires you to love Him supremely, and your neighbor as yourself—to keep the Sabbath day holy—to search the Scriptures—and bring up your children with respect for His laws, and to worship no other God but Him.

But slavery sets all these at nought, and hurls defiance in the face of Jehovah. The forlorn condition in which you are placed does not destroy your obligation to God. You are not certain of heaven, because you allow yourselves to remain in a state of slavery, where you cannot obey the commandments of the Sovereign of the universe. If the ignorance of slavery is a passport to heaven, then it is a blessing, and no curse, and you should rather desire its perpetuity than its abolition. God will not receive slavery, nor ignorance, nor any other state of mind, for love and obedience to Him. Your condition does not **absolve** you from your moral obligation. The diabolical injustice by which your liberties are **cloven** down, NEITHER GOD NOR ANGELS, OR JUST MEN, COMMAND YOU TO SUFFER FOR A SINGLE MOMENT. THEREFORE, IT IS YOUR SOLEMN AND IMPERATIVE DUTY TO USE EVERY MEANS, BOTH MORAL, INTELLECTUAL, AND PHYSICAL, THAT PROMISES SUCCESS.

If a band of heathen men should attempt to enslave a race of Christians, and to place their children under the influence of some false religion, surely Heaven would frown upon the men who would not resist such aggression, even to death. If, on the other hand, a band of Christians should attempt to enslave a race of heathen men, and to entail slavery upon them, and to keep heathenism in the midst of Christianity, the God of heaven would smile upon every effort which the injured might make to **disenthral** themselves.

Brethren, it is wrong for your lordly oppressors to keep you in slavery as it was for the man thief to steal our ancestors from the coast of Africa. You should therefore now use the

absolve: set free, excuse.
cloven: torn, split.
disenthral: free.

Uprisings against Slavery in the South

Garnet's call to slaves in the South to revolt was by no means a new idea to them. There had been more small uprisings on southern plantations than southerners cared to acknowledge. But it was very difficult for slaves to organize into groups because they were generally not permitted to congregate without supervision, nor were they allowed enough time free from work to formulate plans. Two of the better-known plans for revolt, those of Denmark Vesey and Nat Turner—both Christian preachers—demonstrate that many angry and abused slaves of the nineteenth century were more than ready to overthrow the slave owners. These attempts also show how dangerous it was for them to communicate their plans and how swift, sure, and deadly were the reprisals for rebelling.

Denmark Vesey was a freed slave and a minister of the African Methodist Church in Charleston, South Carolina. In 1822 he organized a slave insurrection, basing his plan on the successful slave revolt in Saint-Domingue (now Haiti) in 1791, in which the slaves overthrew the French and set up a prosperous independent government. In his sermons, Vesey urged his congregation to break free from the bonds of slavery and provided Bible passages to support the cause of freedom. He traveled to plantations and spoke to people in the street about his plan for a war of liberation. It is estimated that he recruited nine thousand people to join his revolt. Because so many people knew about the plan, though, the authorities were alerted before it could take place. Vesey and thirty-five of his followers were hanged; forty-three others were deported.

Nine years later, in 1831, Nat Turner, a slave in Southampton County, Virginia, led a three-day uprising. Turner was a self-taught preacher who was viewed by many fellow slaves as a prophet. Turner himself believed he had been called upon by God to free his people. Knowing what had happened to Vesey, Turner kept quiet about his plans to overthrow the slave owners, beginning his revolt with only a few trusted friends. This small group attacked plantations one at a time, killing the slave owners and gathering recruits from among the plantation slaves as they went. His band quickly grew in number to about sixty people, and among them they killed between fifty-five and sixty-five white people on surrounding plantations. On the third day of the uprising the white militia seized Turner's forces, but Turner managed to escape and remained at large for nearly two months. While the militia searched for Turner they killed about two hundred black people. After the rebel leader was caught and hanged, Virginia passed laws making it illegal for slaves to be taught to read or write or to hold religious meetings without a white person present.

same manner of resistance as would have been just in our ancestors when the bloody footprints of the first remorseless soul-thief was placed upon the shores of our fatherland. The humblest peasant is as free in the sight of God as the proudest monarch that ever swayed a sceptre. Liberty is a spirit sent out from God, and like its great Author, is no respecter of persons.

Brethren, the time has come when you must act for yourselves. It is an old and true saying that, "if hereditary bondmen would be free, they must themselves strike the blow." You can plead your own cause, and do the work of emancipation better than any others.

The nations of the Old World are moving in the great cause of universal freedom, and some of them at least will, ere long, do you justice. The combined powers of Europe have placed their broad seal of **disapprobation** upon the African slave-trade.

But in the slaveholding parts of the United States the trade is as brisk as ever. They buy and sell you as though you were brute beasts. The North has done much—her opinion of slavery in the abstract is known. But in regard to the South, we adopt the opinion of the *New York Evangelist*—"We have advanced so far, that the cause apparently waits for a more effectual door to be thrown open than has been yet."

We are about to point you to that more effectual door. Look around you, and behold the bosoms of your loving wives heaving with untold agonies! Hear the cries of your poor children! Remember the stripes your fathers bore. Think of your wretched sisters, loving virtue and purity, as they are driven into **concubinage** and are exposed to the unbridled lusts of **incarnate** devils. Think of the undying glory that hangs around the ancient name of Africa—and forget not that you are native-born American citizens, and as such you are justly entitled to all the rights that are granted to the freest. Think how many tears you have poured out upon the soil which you have cultivated with unrequited toil and enriched with your blood; and then go to your lordly enslavers and tell them plainly, that you are determined to be free. Appeal to their sense of justice, and tell them that they have no more right to oppress you than you have to enslave them. Entreat them to remove the grievous burdens which they have imposed upon you, and to **remunerate** you for your labor.

Promise them renewed diligence in the cultivation of the soil, if they will render to you an equivalent for your services. Point them to the increase of happiness and prosperity in the

disapprobation: disapproval.

concubinage: serving as the mistress of a man one is not married to.

incarnate: given physical (especially human) form and nature.

remunerate: pay, reward.

British West Indies since the Act of Emancipation. Tell them in language which they cannot misunderstand of the exceeding sinfulness of slavery, and of a future judgment, and of the righteous retributions of an indignant God. Inform them that all you desire is FREEDOM, and that nothing else will suffice.

Do this, and forever after cease to toil for the heartless tyrants, who give you no other reward but stripes and abuse. If they then commence work of death, they, and not you, will be responsible for the consequences. You had far better all die—die immediately, than live slaves, and entail your wretchedness upon your posterity. If you would be free in this generation, here is your only hope. However much you and all of us may desire it, there is not much hope of redemption without the shedding of blood. If you must bleed, let it all come at once—rather die freemen than live to be the slaves.

It is impossible, like the children of Israel, to make a grand exodus from the land of bondage. The Pharaohs are on both sides of the blood-red waters! You cannot move en masse to the dominions of the British queen—nor can you pass through Florida and overrun Texas, and at last find peace in Mexico. The propagators of American slavery are spending their blood and treasure that they may plant the black flag in the heart of Mexico and riot in the halls of the Montezumas....

You will not be compelled to spend much time in order to become **inured** to hardships. From the first moment that you breathed the air of heaven, you have been accustomed to nothing else but hardships. The heroes of the American Revolution were never put upon harder fare than a peck of corn and few herrings per week. You have not become **enervated** by the luxuries of life. Your sternest energies have been beaten out upon the anvil of severe trial. Slavery has done this to make you subservient to its own purposes; but it has done more than this, it has prepared you for any emergency. If you receive good treatment, it is what you can hardly expect; if you meet with pain, sorrow, and even death, these are the common lot of the slaves.

Fellowmen! Patient sufferers! Behold your dearest rights crushed to the earth! See your sons murdered, and your wives, mothers and sisters doomed to prostitution. In the name of the merciful God, and by all that life is worth, let it

inured: used to, familiar with.

enervated: weakened.

no longer be a debatable question, whether it is better to choose liberty or death....

Those who have fallen in freedom's conflict, their memories will be cherished by the true-hearted and the God-fearing in all future generations; those who are living, their names are surrounded by a halo of glory.

Brethren, arise, arise! Strike for your lives and liberties. Now is the day and the hour. Let every slave throughout the land do this, and the days of slavery are numbered. You cannot be more oppressed than you have been—you cannot suffer greater cruelties than you have already. Rather die freemen than live to be slaves. Remember that you are FOUR MILLIONS!

It is in your power so to torment the God-cursed slaveholders that they will be glad to let you go free. If the scale was turned, and black men were the masters and white men the slaves, every destructive agent and element would be employed to lay the oppressor low. Danger and death would hang over their heads day and night. Yes, the tyrants would meet with plagues more terrible than those of Pharaoh. But you are a patient people. You act as though your daughters were born to pamper the lusts of your masters and overseers. And worse than all, you tamely submit while your lords tear your wives from your embraces and **defile** them before your eyes. In the name of God, we ask, are you men? Where is the blood of your fathers? Has it all run out of your veins? Awake, awake; millions of voices are calling you! Your dead fathers speak to you from their graves. Heaven, as with a voice of thunder, calls on you to arise from the dust.

Let your motto be resistance! Resistance! RESISTANCE! No oppressed people have ever secured their liberty without resistance. What kind of resistance you had better make you must decide by the circumstances that surround you, and according to the suggestion of **expediency.** Brethren, adieu! Trust in the living God. Labor for the peace of the human race, and remember that you are FOUR MILLIONS!

defile: disgrace, degrade.

expediency: capable of being carried out quickly and efficiently.

" "

Henry Highland Garnet

When the Thirteenth Amendment to the Constitution was ratified in December 1865, slavery was finally abolished throughout the United States. Earlier that year, on February 12, Garnet became the first African American to speak in the U.S. Capitol when he gave a sermon to commemorate the passage of the Thirteenth Amendment in both houses of Congress.

Sources

Aptheker, Herbert, editor, *A Documentary History of the Negro People in the United States,* Volume 1: *From Colonial Times through the Civil War,* Citadel Press, 1965.

Bracey, John H., Jr., August Meier, and Elliott Rudwick, *Black Nationalism in America,* Bobbs-Merrill, 1970.

Dunbar, Alice Moore, editor, *Masterpieces of Negro Eloquence,* Bookery Publishing Company, 1914, reprinted, Johnson Reprint, 1970.

Foner, Philip S., editor, *The Voice of Black America: Major Speeches by Negroes in the United States, 1797-1971,* Simon & Schuster, 1972.

Golden, James L., and Richard D. Rieke, *The Rhetoric of Black Americans,* Charles E. Merrill, 1971.

Ofari, Earl, *"Let Your Motto Be Resistance": The Life and Thought of Henry Highland Garnet,* Beacon, 1972.

Smith, Arthur L., and Stephen Robb, editors, *The Voice of Black Rhetoric: Selections,* Allyn & Bacon, 1971.

Periodicals

Central States Speech Journal, "Henry Highland Garnet: Black Revolutionary in Sheep's Vestments," summer, 1970, pp. 93-98.

Journal of Black Studies, "The Rhetoric of Black Violence in the Antebellum Period: Henry Highland Garnet," September 1971, pp. 45-56.

South Speech Journal, "Nineteenth Century Black Militant: Henry Highland Garnet's Address to the Slaves," fall, 1970, pp. 11-21.

Marcus Garvey

1887–1940

Activist and black nationalist leader

During the late 1910s and early 1920s, Marcus Garvey became the first man to speak for millions of blacks all over the world as the founder and head of the Universal Negro Improvement Association (UNIA). The UNIA blended the self-help teachings of **Booker T. Washington** (see entry) and Garvey's own dreams of an "Africa for Africans." The organization's message was especially appealing to the frustrated and disappointed black veterans of World War I. They had returned home in triumph only to find that their sacrifices on the battlefields of Europe did not earn them equality in America. Garvey responded to their discontent with his own form of **black nationalism.** He urged blacks to take pride in their racial heritage and look to Africa as the place to establish a new homeland that would be free of inequality and prejudice.

Early Life

The youngest of eleven children, Garvey was born on the Caribbean island of Jamaica. He attended school until the *age of fourteen, then went to work as a printer's apprentice. He remained active in the printing trade for several years before setting off on a series of travels that would change the course of his life.*

In Garvey's native Jamaica, blacks had long suffered under British colonial rule. People of African descent faced similar difficulties on neighboring Caribbean islands and throughout Latin America. Having noticed oppressive conditions during his visits to various countries in Central and South America, Garvey began to think about the treatment of blacks in other parts of the world. In 1912, he went to England for a period of extensive study of Africa and colonialism (the policy of a government to acquire or rule over foreign territories). Returning to Jamaica in 1914, he established the Universal Negro Improvement and Conservation Association (later shortened to the Universal Negro Improvement Association) and African Communities League. His goal, he announced, was to "lift the race" and establish a politically and economically independent black nation in Africa.

Moves UNIA Headquarters to the United States

Eager to reach an international audience with his ideas, Garvey headed to New York City in 1916. There he set up a branch of the UNIA and launched a weekly newspaper, Negro World. *A persuasive speaker with a flamboyant personality, he had little trouble attracting thousands of supporters to his colorful parades and rallies in the Harlem neighborhood of the city. Before long, the UNIA became the center of a growing empire that included several publications and numerous businesses. Among the UNIA's most famous commercial enterprises was the Black Star Line of steamships, which was supposed to encourage links (especially business-related ones) between black people worldwide. By the early 1920s, the movement claimed to have about one to two million followers who were convinced that separation rather than integration was the key to black success and happiness.*

On November 25, 1922, Garvey spoke to a gathering in New York City about the principles of the UNIA and what it

black nationalism: a belief that blacks should separate from whites and form their own self-governing communities and businesses.

hoped to accomplish. An excerpt from his remarks is reprinted here from Philosophy and Opinions of Marcus Garvey, *compiled by Amy Jacques Garvey, Universal Publishing House, Volume 1, 1923, Volume 2, 1925, both volumes reprinted, Arno, 1969.*

❝

Over five years ago the Universal Negro Improvement Association placed itself before the world as the movement through which the new and rising Negro would give expression of his feelings. This Association adopts an attitude not of hostility to other races and peoples of the world, but an attitude of self-respect, of manhood rights on behalf of four hundred million Negroes of the world.

We represent peace, harmony, love, human sympathy, human rights and human justice, and that is why we fight so much. Wheresoever human rights are denied to any group, wheresoever justice is denied to any group, there the UNIA finds a cause. And at this time among all the peoples of the world, the group that suffers most from injustice, the group that is denied most of those rights that belong to all humanity, is the black group of four hundred million. Because of that injustice, because of that denial of our rights, we go forth under the leadership of the One who is always on the side of right to fight the common cause of humanity; to fight as we fought in the Revolutionary War, as we fought in the Civil War, as we fought in the Spanish-American War, and as we fought in the war between 1914-18 [World War I] on the battle plains of France and Flanders. As we fought up the heights of Mesopotamia; even so under the leadership of the UNIA, we are marshaling the four hundred million Negroes of the world to fight for the emancipation of the race and for the redemption of the country of our fathers.

We represent a new line of thought among Negroes.... We of the UNIA believe that what is good for the other fellow is good for us. If government is something that is worthwhile; if government is something that is appreciable and helpful and protective to others, then we also want to experiment in government. We do not mean a government that will make

us citizens without rights or subjects without consideration. We mean the kind of government that will place our race in control, even as other races are in control of their own governments.

That does not suggest anything that is unreasonable. It was not unreasonable for George Washington, the great hero and father of the country, to have fought for the freedom of

America giving to us this great republic and this great democracy; it was not unreasonable for the liberals of France to have fought against the monarchy to give to the world French democracy and French republicanism; it was no **unrighteous** cause that led in giving to the world the social democracy of Russia.... It is therefore not an unrighteous cause for the UNIA to lead four hundred million Negroes all over the world to fight for the liberation of our country....

In **advocating** the principles of this Association we find we have been very much misunderstood and very much misrepresented by men from within our own race, as well as others from without.... Those who probably would have taken kindly notice of this great movement, have been led to believe that this movement seeks, not to develop the good within the race, but to give expression to that which is most destructive and most harmful to society and to government.

I desire to remove the misunderstanding that has been created in the minds of millions of peoples throughout the world in their relationship to the organization. The Universal Negro Improvement Association stands for the Bigger Brotherhood; the Universal Negro Improvement Association stands for human rights, not only for Negroes, but for all races. The Universal Negro Improvement Association believes in the rights of not only the black race, but the white race, the yellow race and the brown race. The Universal Negro Improvement Association believes that the white man has as much right to be considered, the yellow man has as much right to be considered, the brown man has as much right to be considered as well as the black man of Africa.

In view of the fact that the black man of Africa has contributed as much to the world as the white man of Europe, and the brown man and yellow man of Asia, we of the Universal Negro Improvement Association demand that the white, yellow and brown races give to the black man his place in the civilization of the world. We ask for nothing more than the rights of four hundred million Negroes. We are not seeking, as I said before, to destroy or disrupt the society or the government of other races, but we are determined that four hundred million of us shall unite ourselves to free our motherland from the grasp of the invader. We of the Universal Negro Improvement Association are determined to

unrighteous: unjust, unfair.
advocating: promoting, supporting.

Marcus Garvey

unite four hundred million Negroes for their own industrial, political, social and religious emancipation.

We of the Universal Negro Improvement Association are determined to unite the four hundred million Negroes of the world to give expression to their own feeling; we are determined to unite the four hundred million Negroes of the world for the purpose of building a civilization of their own.... We are looking toward political freedom on the continent of Africa, the land of our fathers....

The Universal Negro Improvement Association is not seeking to disrupt any organized system of government, but the Association is determined to bring Negroes together for the building up of a nation of their own. And why? Because we have been forced to it. We have been forced to it throughout the world; not only in America, not only in Europe, not only in the British Empire, but wheresoever the black man happens to find himself, he has been forced to do for himself.

To talk about government is a little more than some of our people can appreciate just at this time. The average man does not think that way, just because he finds himself a citizen or a subject of some country.... But we of the UNIA have studied seriously this question of nationality among Negroes—this American nationality, this British nationality, this French, Italian or Spanish nationality, and have discovered that it counts for **nought** when that nationality comes in conflict with the racial idealism of the group that rules. When our interests clash with those of the ruling faction, then we find that we have absolutely no rights.

In times of peace, when everything is all right, Negroes have a hard time, wherever we go, wheresoever we find ourselves, getting those rights that belong to us, in common with others whom we claim as fellow citizens; getting that consideration that should be ours by right of the constitution, by right of the law; but in the time of trouble they make us all partners in the cause, as happened in the last war [World War I], when we were partners, whether British, French or American Negroes. And we were told that we must forget everything in an effort to save the nation.

We have saved many nations in this manner, and we have lost our lives doing that before. Hundreds of thousands—nay,

nought: nothing.

Black Troops in World War I

When the United States entered World War I in 1917, blacks responded with enthusiasm to President Woodrow Wilson's request that all Americans do their part to help "make the world safe for democracy." Besides the many thousands who braved discrimination and outright hostility to work in the defense industry, four hundred thousand African American men served in the armed forces. The majority were assigned to dock-managing units at ports or labor units as quartermaster troops. Racism and racial stereotyping were strong factors in the military at the time, where Jim Crow policies were the standard.

The U.S. War Department initially ignored demands that blacks be trained as commissioned officers, but initiatives by the National Association for the Advancement of Colored People, the Urban League, and several black newspapers necessitated a change in policy; an all-black Officer Training School was established at Fort Dodge, Iowa. The school graduated and commissioned 639 black officers in 1917. This posed a problem for the War Department, which had an iron-clad rule that no black officer could command white officers or enlisted men.

The War Department found a solution: It "attached" several black regiments to the allied French Army, basically abandoning the officers it had trained. One of these groups, the 369th Infantry Regiment, established the best World War I record of any U.S. Army infantry regiment. The 369th served for 191 consecutive days in the trenches and never lost a foot of ground to the Germans. The regiment, sometimes called the "Harlem Hell Fighters," won its laurels attached to the French 4th Army, using French weapons and wearing U.S. uniforms. Black soldiers in general earned an impressive number of awards in World War I for their combat bravery.

After the war, African Americans who had served on behalf of the United States expected their government and its citizens to live by the principles they all had supposedly fought for in Europe. Black veterans assumed the American society would reward their hard work and sacrifices overseas with equality and goodwill at home. Instead the racial climate in the United States took a turn for the worse during the late 1910s and 1920s. A series of deadly and destructive riots rocked the nation and the number of lynchings sharply increased. Frustrated and deeply disillusioned, many African Americans looked to black separatist movements such as the UNIA as their only hope for a better future.

millions of black men, lie buried under the ground due to that old-time camouflage of saving the nation.... All that we have received for what we have done, even in giving up our lives, is just what you are receiving now, just what I am receiving now.

You and I fare no better in America, in the British empire,

or in any other part of the white world; we fare no better than any black man wheresoever he shows his head. And why? Because we have been satisfied to allow ourselves to be led, educated, to be directed by the other fellow, who has always sought to lead in the world in that direction that would satisfy him and strengthen his position. We have allowed ourselves for the last five hundred years to be a race of followers, following every race that has led in the direction that would make them more secure.

The UNIA is reversing the old-time order of things. We refuse to be followers any more. We are leading ourselves. That means, if any saving is to be done, later on, whether it is saving this one nation or that one government, we are going to seek a method of saving Africa first....

The difference between the Universal Negro Improvement Association and the other movements of this country, and probably the world, is that the Universal Negro Improvement Association seeks independence of government, while the other organizations seek to make the Negro a secondary part of existing governments.... If the black man is to reach the height of his ambition in this country—if the black man is to get all of his constitutional rights in America—then the black man should have the same chance in the nation as any other man to become president of the nation, or a street cleaner in New York....

Are they prepared to give us such political equality? You and I can live in the United States of America for one hundred more years, and our generations may live for two hundred years or for five thousand more years, and so long as there is a black and white population, when the majority is on the side of the white race, you and I will never get political justice or get political equality in this country.

Then why should a black man with rising ambition, after preparing himself in every possible way to give expression to that highest ambition, allow himself to be kept down by racial prejudice within a country? If I am as educated as the next man, if I am as prepared as the next man, if I have passed through the best schools and colleges and universities as the other fellow, why should I not have a fair chance to compete with the other fellow for the biggest position in the nation? I have feelings, I have blood, I have senses like the other fellow; I have ambition, I have hope. Why should he, because of some racial prejudice, keep me down and why should I concede to him the right to rise above me, and to establish himself as my permanent master?

That is where the UNIA differs from other organizations. I refuse to **stultify** my ambition, and every true Negro refuses to stultify his ambition to suit any one, and therefore the UNIA decides if America is not big enough for two presidents ... then we are not going to quarrel over the matter.... Hence, the Universal Negro Improvement Association does not seek to interfere with [existing] social and political systems ..., but by the arrangement of things today the UNIA refuses to recognize any political or social system in Africa except that which we are about to establish for ourselves.

We are not preaching a propaganda of hate against anybody. We love the white man; we love all humanity, because we feel that we cannot live without the other. The white man is as necessary to the existence of the Negro as the Negro is necessary to his existence. There is a common relationship that we cannot escape....

The question often asked is what does it require to redeem a race and free a country? If it takes manpower, if it takes scientific intelligence, if it takes education of any kind, or if it takes blood, then the four hundred million Negroes of the world have it....

If we have been liberal minded enough to give our life's blood in France, in Mesopotamia and elsewhere, fighting for the white man, whom we have always assisted, surely we have not forgotten to fight for ourselves, and when the time comes that the world will again give Africa an opportunity for freedom, surely four hundred million black men will march out on the battle plains of Africa, under the colors of the red, the black and the green.

We shall march out, yes, as black American citizens, as black British subjects, as black French citizens, as black Italians or as black Spaniards, but we shall march out with a greater loyalty, the loyalty of race. We shall march out in answer to the cry of our fathers, who cry out to us for the redemption of our own country, our motherland, Africa.

stultify: restrain.

We shall march out, not forgetting the blessings of America. We shall march out, not forgetting the blessings of civilization. We shall march out with a history of peace before and behind us, and surely that history shall be our breastplate, for how can man fight better than knowing that the cause for which he fights is righteous? How can man fight more gloriously than by knowing that behind him is a history of slavery, a history of bloody **carnage** and massacre inflicted upon a race because of its inability to protect itself and fight? Shall we not fight for the glorious opportunity of protecting and forever more establishing ourselves as a mighty race and nation, never more to be disrespected by men? Glorious shall be the battle when the time comes to fight for our people and our race.

We should say to the millions who are in Africa to hold the fort, for we are coming four hundred million strong.

99

In 1925, Garvey was sentenced to five years in jail for mail fraud. The charges stemmed from his efforts to raise money for the Black Star Line and other UNIA businesses, most of which had experienced major financial problems in the early 1920s. Two years into his sentence, he was pardoned by President Calvin Coolidge and then deported to Jamaica.

*Without the force of Garvey's charismatic leadership, however, the UNIA had fallen apart while he was in jail. Try as he might, he could not regain the influence he had once enjoyed. Eventually, he moved to England, where he died a forgotten man. But many of Garvey's ideas—especially about black pride—lived on in the philosophies of future black nationalists such as **Malcolm X** (see entry) and the Black Panthers (see entries on **Stokely Carmichael** and **Eldridge Cleaver**).*

Sources

Books

Boulware, Marcus H., *The Oratory of Negro Leaders: 1900–1968*, Negro Universities Press, 1969.

carnage: killing.

Clarke, John Henrik, editor, *Marcus Garvey and the Vision of Africa,* Vintage, 1974.

Cronon, Edmund David, *Black Moses: The Story of Marcus Garvey and the Universal Negro Improvement Association,* revised edition, University of Wisconsin Press, 1987.

Duffy, Bernard K., and Halford R. Ryan, editors, *American Orators of the Twentieth Century: Critical Studies and Sources,* Greenwood Press, 1987.

Foner, Philip S., editor, *The Voice of Black America: Major Speeches by Negroes in the United States, 1797–1971,* Simon & Schuster, 1972.

Garvey, Amy Jacques, compiler, *Philosophy and Opinions of Marcus Garvey,* Universal Publishing House, Volume 1, 1923, Volume 2, 1925, both volumes reprinted, Arno, 1969.

Hill, Robert A., editor, *Marcus Garvey and the Universal Negro Improvement Association Papers,* three volumes, University of California Press, 1975.

Hill, Roy L., *Rhetoric of Racial Revolt,* Golden Bell Press, 1964.

Meltzer, Milton, editor, *The Black Americans: A History in Their Own Words, 1619–1983,* Crowell, 1984.

O'Neill, Daniel J., editor, *Speeches by Black Americans,* Dickenson, 1971.

Smith, Arthur L., *Rhetoric of Black Revolution,* Allyn & Bacon, 1969.

Smith, Arthur L., and Stephen Robb, editors, *The Voice of Black Rhetoric: Selections,* Allyn & Bacon, 1971.

Stein, Judith, *The World of Marcus Garvey: Race and Class in Modern Society,* Louisiana State University Press, 1986.

Alex Haley

1921–1992
Writer

Alex Haley was the author of the award-winning 1976 best-seller Roots: The Saga of an American Family. *This fascinating story of a black man's attempt to trace his genealogy (the record of a person's or a family's ancestry) touched the lives of millions throughout the world, especially after it became the basis for two popular television miniseries. As a result of Haley's work, many Americans—including record numbers of black Americans—were inspired to research their own family histories.* Roots*'s harsh portrayal of slavery and its aftermath also shed new light and intensified public attention on modern race relations. It also showed both black and white Americans how closely their pasts have been linked over the last several hundred years.*

Early Life

The son of a professor and a teacher, Alex Haley was born in Ithaca, New York. Although he lived in various college towns throughout the South while growing up, he also

"THERE WERE A NUMBER OF ROCKING CHAIRS ON THE FRONT PORCH.... THE SISTERS WOULD GET IN THE ROCKING CHAIRS, AND I WOULD GET BEHIND MY GRANDMOTHER'S ROCKING CHAIR.... AND THEY WOULD TALK ABOUT THEIR GIRLHOOD."

spent a great deal of time at his grandparents' home in Henning, Tennessee. There he first heard the name of his African ancestor, Kunta Kinte, who had been kidnapped, sold into slavery, and brought to the United States some-time during the late 1700s. As they relaxed together on the front porch on summer evenings, Haley's grandmother and her sisters told story after story about Kunte Kinte and his descendants. These stories later formed the basis of Roots.

At the age of eighteen Haley began a twenty-year career with the Coast Guard. During the long, lonely weeks at sea, he started writing and when he retired in 1959, he decided to become a professional writer. After struggling for a time to get his work published, success came in the form of regu-lar assignments for major magazines. Interview work with Playboy *led to his biggest break. After interviewing* **Malcolm X** *(see entry) for the magazine, Haley was chosen to help the Black Muslim leader write his life story. They fin-ished the project just days before Malcolm X was assassi-nated.* The Autobiography of Malcolm X *was published later that year (1965) and has been a steady best-seller ever since.*

After he wrapped up his work on Malcolm X's autobiog-raphy, Haley began collecting material on the history of his own family. Over the course of about nine years, whenever he had a break between writing assignments, he visited libraries and other research centers. He also made a trip to a village in Gambia, the African homeland of his ancestors. There he listened to the local griot, *or oral historian, tell the tale of a young man named Kinte who had left the vil-lage one day to chop wood and was never seen again.*

To Haley's surprise, the story he heard that day was very much like the ones he used to listen to on his grandmother's front porch back in Tennessee. Could they possibly be about the same person? And how did everything fit together with the other information he had gathered on his family?

Finding the answers to those and other questions was a project far bigger and more complicated than anything Haley had ever tackled before. It was an emotional struggle at times, too, because he felt a duty to his ancestors and to all African Americans to try to give others a sense of the horrors they had endured under slavery. In the end, Haley chose to blend elements of fact and fiction to create a dramatic yet basically truthful story. The result was Roots, *which vividly brought to life the realities of slavery and its impact on several generations of a black American family.*

Achieves Worldwide Fame

Roots *was tremendously successful with readers as well as critics. It zoomed to the top of the best-seller list and won a number of important honors, including a special Pulitzer Prize and a National Book Award. The television miniseries, which was broadcast in 1977, was watched by two-thirds of the possible viewing audience (a record at the time). A sequel that was shown in 1979 also proved to be very popular. One of the things that made the miniseries so revolutionary was that it dramatized what it might feel like to be a slave from a black rather than a white perspective.*

Overwhelmed by the attention he received as the author of Roots, *Haley found it difficult for a while to return to his writing. He eventually did so but still enjoyed an extremely busy second career appearing on television and radio programs and lecturing to all kinds of audiences throughout the world.*

One of these lectures was on January 30, 1992, at Hope College in Holland, Michigan. There Haley shared with more than a thousand people one of his favorite stories— how Roots *came to be. The following is a transcription of part of his speech taken from a tape recording provided by the Hope College Collection of the Joint Archives of Holland.*

...I was raised in a little town called Henning, Tennessee. H-E-double N-I-N-G. It's in the western part of the state, about fifty miles north of Memphis. The population when I was there—as a boy, anyway—was about 470 people, about half and half white and black. It was another little typical farming town ... where the church and the school just about ran [everything]....

I was raised, as we say in the South, by my grandparents. I had a particular love for my grandparents. Not that I didn't love my parents—they both were teachers, but their being teachers had them away from the home more than normally might have been the case....

My grandfather ... owned a little lumberyard in this little town, which was unusual [in] that there would be a black owner of a lumberyard.... And he was very highly respected. For me, he was just the utter end of macho, and utter end of somebody to be proud of, and [a] role model. He was tall, straight, black....

It was being raised like this, by loving grandparents whom I loved in turn—and then all of a relative sudden, my beloved grandfather died. It was as if the bottom fell out of everything. Nobody could *believe* that Will Palmer was gone.

Afterwards, Grandma sat like a zombie on the front porch in a white wicker rocking chair. People would pass on the road, and they would speak to her, "How're you, Miz Sis?"— her name was Cynthia, and people called her Sis—and Grandma often wouldn't even acknowledge the greetings. Nobody seemed to mind, because people knew how grief-stricken she was. And then, even I, a little boy of five, could tell that Grandma was going under if she didn't do *something*.

And after a while, she *did* do something. She began to write letters, more letters than I ever had known her to write—a total of five. And she wrote them in one week, one per afternoon. And she was writing them to her sisters, who lived in various very exotic places like East St. Louis; like Detroit; Inkster, Michigan, was another one. She was asking her sisters if they would come and spend the next summer there with us. One by one, the sisters answered, and they said they would be coming.... Within the space of about ten days, five sisters came from all these glamorous, exotic places.

They spent the days, for the better part, visiting people around in Henning whom they had known growing up there as young girls before they got married and went away. Then in the evening, we would all come together and we would have what they called supper.... And then the sisters would just kind of trickle toward the front porch. By now, it would be early night.

There were a number of rocking chairs on the front porch. Around three sides of the porch were thick honeysuckle vines…. And then over the honeysuckle were thousands, I guess, of what we called lightning bugs, fireflies, flicking on and off. And the sisters would get in the rocking chairs, and I would get behind my grandmother's rocking chair….

And there would occur two things that the sisters all did that I know they never once thought about. It was purely involuntary, just automatic; it was what you did on front porches in the South at that time. The first thing there in the early dark, they would take maybe five minutes to get their rocking together. You know, you don't just sit down and start rocking. You've got to get that chair at just the right angle for you, and then you've got to get the **cadence** just right….

And once they got their rocking kind of synchronized, every single one of them—without thinking about it, I know, they just did it—would run their hand in their apron pocket and come up with a little cylindrical tin can of sweet … snuff. And they would pull out this lower lip and kind of load it up, and then they would start taking little practice shots out over the honeysuckle vine. The champion in that group among the sisters without any question was my Great-Aunt Liz, who had come from somewhere called Okmulgee, Oklahoma, where she'd been teaching for more than twenty-five years. Aunt Liz, when she was in good form, could drop a lightning bug at four yards. She was just incredible!

This was really what kind of established what might be called the ambience of the evening. They would start now laughing, there in the dark, me listening, ears like saucers. Not that I felt there was any particular value—it was just fascinating to listen. And they would talk about their girlhood. One of the things that got to me was how they would sort of slap each other on the thigh or the shoulder, and they'd say, "Oh, girl!" I remember thinking to myself, "These are gray-haired women calling each other 'girl.' It's terrible!" I didn't have the insight, of course, to know that they were reminiscing and as such they *were* girls again….

And then they'd begin to talk about their parents. They loved to talk about their father—strict, strong, blacksmith Tom Murray, who had been a slave blacksmith and who had

cadence: rhythm.

vowed during slavery that come freedom he would own his own shop, as he in fact later had there in the town of Henning. And they talked about their mother, her name Arrena. They used to love to talk about how she would get upset if anybody called her "Irene," as people would sometimes do. And she would make certain that they understood her name was properly spelled A-R-R-E-N-A, and that she was one-fourth Cherokee Indian.

And then they would eventually start waggling their heads and cluck-clucking and saying something like, "Oh, he was just scandalous!" And when I began to hear this, I knew they were getting ready now to lay into their daddy's daddy. And this was the one that they talked about who fought roosters who was called Chicken George. They loved to talk about what a sinner he was. He drank whiskey, which was sinful, and when he drank he would curse (that was the first time I ever heard the expression "taking the Lord's name in vain"), and then there was another sin of his that I gathered—I didn't know what it meant, but from the way they acted I gathered it must have been worse than the other two combined—and that was womanizing, and they said he was doing that all the time.

And then their whole manner would change. All these people up to this time they had talked about had lived in somewhere called Alamance County, North Carolina. Now they became quiet, all but reverent, as they talked about Chicken George's mother. And they said she lived not in Alamance County, North Carolina, but in Spotsylvania County, Virginia. She lived on the plantation of her master, who was a medical doctor. His name [was] Dr. William Waller, and he was called Mas' Waller. And they told how he had a cook named Bell who was the mother of Miss Kizzy, who was the mother of Chicken George.

The father of Miss Kizzy was this African who was a buggy driver for the master. They told how the African drove the master both on his medical rounds and his social rounds. And then they told how when Miss Kizzy was coming up as a little girl, the African, when he got a chance taking her around, would hold her hand and he would, as best he could, convey to his little daughter sounds. He would point out tree, rock, cow—things, simple things like that, and he would say to her the African word, the word from his country and his people that meant that thing. And Miss Kizzy began to learn a few phonetic sounds.

She grew on up, building a little bit better repertoire of these sounds and eventually a few stories that he could tell her, in a very halting way with what little English he had commanded, about his country, where he came from, things like that. And then when Miss Kizzy was fifteen she was sold away. She was sold to a man whose name was Tom Lea, L-E-A. And as it would turn out, it was Tom Lea who became the father of Miss Kizzy's first child, a boy who was given the name George. And it was George who grew up into the rooster fighter, the gamecock fighter Chicken George.

Chicken George, for all his womanizing, did marry—or, in slave terms, he jumped the broom, that was the practice at that time for marrying among them—with Matilda, and in time, Matilda gave birth to eight children. The youngest of them, the second youngest of them, a boy named Tom, when he got to be fifteen, was apprenticed to a Dutch blacksmith. And Tom became an outstanding young slave blacksmith. In time, Tom met a young slave maid named Arrena, who was at the Holt plantation in Alamance County. And they jumped the broom. And in time, Arrena gave birth to seven children, all girls.

And now, two generations later, there were the five remaining ones of those girls sitting on the front porch of my grandmother, whom they called—and I couldn't understand that, they called her "the baby," and I couldn't figure how in the world is anybody's grandma "the baby"—and they were talking and they were reminiscing and they were telling the stories and I was listening. None of us had any idea that what we really were participating in was something which nowadays in more informed circles we call "oral history"—the passing down of the story from the elder to the younger. But I grew up hearing those stories, learning them through repetitive hearing....

And thus, I grew up. I got into other interests. I was in school; I was not a good student. Teachers used to tell my parents that I was a daydreamer, and they could not have been more correct.... My grades used to kind of reflect this.

And my father, who was a teacher, a dean of agriculture, was distressed no end that I was not being a role model for my two younger brothers.

Our father was determined that we were all going to be professors as he was. And when I got such bad grades, I got a good deal of what we'd call corporal punishment.... Finally— I had the kind of dad who when he got something on his mind you heard a lot about it, and he began to talk about maturing. I had needed, he said, to go somewhere which was safe and mature to get enough sense to come back and finish college, then get a master's, get a doctorate, and become a professor as he was.

And so my father went shopping in the military for me. He thought that was the best place. The Army, the Marine Corps, the Navy—all had four-year enlistments. And then he found one we didn't know much of anything about called the United States Coast Guard which had a three-year enlistment, and dad thought three years ought to do it. So with his recommendations, to put it charitably, I jumped into the Coast Guard....

99

At this point, Haley describes his unexpected turn to professional writing during what turned out to be twenty years with the Coast Guard. It began when, to help pass the time (and earn a little extra money) during the long, lonely weeks at sea, he started writing love letters for his less-talented shipmates. Haley soon found that he really enjoyed writing, and as his skills improved, he tried his hand at producing stories and articles. Eventually, he was able to sell some of his pieces to magazines, which gave him the idea that he just might be able to make a living as a writer. So when he retired from the service in 1959, Haley decided to pursue his dream.

After a couple of tough years struggling to get his work published, Haley began to write fairly regularly for several magazines. His biggest break came when editors at Play-boy *approached him about developing a new interview feature. His first subject was jazz trumpeter Miles Davis.*

The piece was so popular that Haley was asked to do more interviews. One of these turned out to be with Nation of Islam spokesman Malcolm X, whom Haley had first met when he wrote an article on the Nation for the Reader's Digest. *The two men got along so well that Malcolm X asked Haley to help him write his life story. They finished the project,* The Autobiography of Malcolm X, *just days before the Black Muslim leader was assassinated.*

❝

When I finished [*The Autobiography of Malcolm X*]—there's a saying in the business that when you've finished a big book, you're kind of like a lady who's just had a baby. Something you were full of, and all of a sudden it's gone, and you don't know what to do with yourself. And in that circumstance, of sorts, I was in Washington one Saturday morning.... I was walking down the sidewalk..., and I saw ahead of me this tall, imposing building. Across the top of the columns was inscribed into the concrete, "Archives of the United States."

...I never will know really what impelled me to go up the steep steps, unless it was that I have always had this innate thing about history. It always has kind of been like a magnet to me. I went up the steps, and in the main reading room, people were kind of moving around among the card indexes that we don't have anymore.... A young fellow, a young white fellow, came up to me, and he really kind of startled me, because I hadn't expected anybody to say anything or pay any attention to me. And he said, "Could I be of help to you?" I don't know why, I just opened my mouth, and out of my mouth came something I don't understand really why it did to this day. I just said to him, "I wonder if I could see the census records for Alamance County, North Carolina, 1870."

Now why that gives me the goosebumps in a way is because I don't believe I had heard or read the words "Alamance County" since I was a boy.... And I said "1870" because somewhere in the interim I had learned that the first time black people were named in the census was after the Civil War, which would have been 1870.

The young man was not taken aback. He said I should go up into the microfilm room, and I did. And he caused to be sent up eight boxes of microfilm. For the first time ever I threaded one of those reels, started one of those reels into one of the viewing machines....

I went through four reels, looking. It was like standing on a hot, dusty road in wherever was Alamance County, North Carolina, looking at the people pass. And then I looked down, and what in the world am I looking at! There is "Murray, Thomas." His age, color—"b" for "black", occupation—blacksmith. For pete's sake! How many times had I heard Grandma, Aunt Liz, Aunt Plus, all of them talk about their daddy, Tom Murray the blacksmith, Alamance County! Could it possibly be that there had been more than one? And then I looked underneath his name, and there is his wife, and what do I see? A-R-R-E-N-A. How many times had I heard them say that mama spelled her name that way?

By now, I'm galvanized. And I'm looking at the names of the children. It wasn't that the names surprised me, because I'd sat on the front porch with these ladies of these names. But what astounded me was the ages—twelve, ten, nine, seven—Aunt Liz, the one I told you about from Oklahoma, the snuff-dipper, no way in the world she could have ever been six years old!—and then I was going down and all of a sudden I just was *enraged!* Where was Cynthia? Where was Grandma? How could they *possibly* have done this and not have Grandma? If it hadn't been for her, I wouldn't be there! I felt like taking the chair I'd been in and smashing the machine!

I remember then—I don't know why, from where, it just kind of trickled up in my head like a bubble might rise in this pitcher of water—*she wasn't born yet.* And when I look back upon it, that had to have been my first bite of what is ... called the genealogical bug, from which there is no cure. Once you have been bitten by it, for the rest of your born days you'll be digging in old musty, dusty piles of records looking for a name, looking for a date, looking for a clue of any sort that will help you reach back with a family that doesn't even have to be your family.

That was the beginning of what would become nine years of researching—not steadily researching, but doing what I could in between doing magazine articles to make a living by. And then, after that was done, three years of writing.

Finally, there was this book. I didn't know what to call it. I always liked one-word titles. I was for a long time, about five years, the title I had in my head was *Before This Anger*. The reason I came on that title was, it was in the sixties, and it was the civil rights struggles and all kinds of upheavals in that interest, and I had met quite a number of what I perceived to be really good, sincere, well-minded, and sympathetic, empathetic white people who had kind of said to me in one or another way, "What happened? Your people have been, you know, so peaceful, and all of a sudden all this upset. What is the trouble?" And so I had kind of thought, well, if I can write a book which would give these and other people some better perception of the history of us, of how we got to be here, and how we developed into whatever we are now, it might give them a better picture. Hence I had come up with this title of *Before This Anger*.

And then it was when I had been writing *The Autobiography of Malcolm X* that just by accident, different chapters—I had a thing about, you know, you write the chapter and then somewhere in the course of it, of that chapter, there is a word that seems to you to capture what that chapter's about....

It was in that way I had gotten to like one word. And I kept thinking word, what word? And somehow by Providence, the word "roots" came to me, and so I changed the title. And I really, truly think that that word has had a lot to do with, for some reason, the success of the book, because it has meaning for everybody. The word "roots" has come to be used since the publication of the book in many, many ways that have nothing to do with the book, but it applies to all of us....

99

Alex Haley's talk at Hope College was one of his last public appearances. Less than two weeks later, while in Seattle, Washington, for yet another speaking engagement, he suffered a fatal heart attack. He was buried on the grounds of his grandparents' home in Tennessee, not far from the front porch where he first heard the story of Kunta Kinte.

About a year before his death, Haley donated most of his papers to the University of Tennessee in Knoxville. After his death, his Malcolm X material was auctioned off to help pay estate debts. Other noteworthy items, including his Pulitzer Prize, his Emmy Award, his typewriter, and various African artifacts, are in storage at the Tennessee State Museum in Nashville. Friends and family hope one day to raise enough money to turn his grandparents' home in Henning into a memorial.

Sources

Books

Dictionary of Literary Biography, Volume 38: *Afro-American Writers After 1955: Dramatists and Prose Writers,* Gale, 1985.

Haley, Alex, with Malcolm X, *The Autobiography of Malcolm X,* Grove, 1965.

Haley, Alex, *Roots: The Saga of an American Family,* Doubleday, 1976.

Haley, Alex, with David Stevens, *Alex Haley's "Queen": The Story of an American Family,* Morrow, 1993.

Periodicals

Detroit News, "Friends Try to Help Museum in Alex Haley's Hometown Take Root," February 11, 1993, p. 7C.

Ebony, "Alex Haley: The Man Behind *Roots,*" April 1977, pp. 33-41; "We Must Honor Our Ancestors," August 1986, reprinted in special issue, November 1990, pp. 152-156.

Grand Rapids Press, "Author Laments Loss of Family Ties," January 31, 1992; "Haley's *Roots* Manuscripts Go on Public View," February 23, 1993, p. D4.

New Republic, "Roots of Victory, Roots of Defeat," March 12, 1977, pp. 27-28.

Newsweek, "In Search of a Heritage," September 27, 1976, pp. 94-96; "After Haley's Comet," February 14, 1977, pp. 97-98; "Uncle Tom's Roots," February 14, 1977, p. 100.

New York Times, October 14, 1976; February 11, 1992, p. B8.

People, March 28, 1977; "Having Left LA to Settle in His Native Tennessee, Alex Haley Turns Out His First Book Since *Roots,*" December 12, 1988, pp. 126-128; "Deep Roots," February 24, 1992; "Torn Up by the Roots: An Estate Auction Threatens to Scatter the Precious Possessions of Alex Haley's Lifetime," October 5, 1992.

Playboy, "In Memoriam," July 1992.

Publishers Weekly, "Alex Haley," September 6, 1976, pp. 8-12.

Reader's Digest, "My Search for Roots: A Black American's Story," April, 1977, pp. 148-152; "What *Roots* Means to Me," May 1977, pp. 73-76.

Time, October 18, 1976; "Why *Roots* Hit Home," February 14, 1977, pp. 69-77; "*Roots'* Roots," December 25, 1978, p. 30; February 24, 1992, p. 68.

Fannie Lou Hamer

1917–1977

Civil rights activist

"I COULD HEAR THE
SOUNDS OF LICKS AND
HORRIBLE SCREAMS...."

To most people, the act of registering to vote is not an especially momentous event. But in 1962 in Fannie Lou Hamer's home state of Mississippi, blacks interested in voting were often greeted with anger, threats, and even violence from some whites. Despite the risks, Hamer and several other volunteers courageously set out to challenge the people who were denying them the chance to vote. What they had to overcome to exercise their constitutional rights is one of the horrifying and yet lesser-known stories of the civil rights movement. And as their leader, Hamer is an often-overlooked figure in the struggle.

Early Life

Hamer was the youngest of twenty children born into a very poor family of sharecroppers in Montgomery County, Mississippi. Sharecroppers are farmers who are given food and a place to live plus credit for seeds and tools in exchange for working someone else's land and sharing the profits from their labors—minus the charges for the supplies they use. For Hamer's family sharecropping was an extremely difficult life; their house was little more than a shack, there was never enough to eat, and there was little hope that things would get any better. Young Fannie Lou began helping in the cotton fields at the age of six. By the age of twelve, she had dropped out of school to work full-time with the rest of her family.

In 1942, Hamer married a man who worked as a tractor driver on a neighboring plantation. She seemed destined to follow in the footsteps of her parents. Yet even then she began to feel a need to do something to help her family and other African Americans—especially Southern blacks—find a way out of poverty and despair.

Tries to Register to Vote

For the next twenty years or so, however, Hamer had to concentrate on making a living. At first, she worked out in the fields. She was then promoted to the less back-breaking (but still low-paying) position of timekeeper. In August 1962, however, she attended her first civil rights meeting. Held in her hometown of Ruleville, it was a joint rally sponsored by the Southern Christian Leadership Conference (SCLC) and the Student Nonviolent Coordinating Committee (SNCC; see box). There she listened to a series of rousing speeches encouraging blacks to challenge Mississippi's unjust voting laws. Inspired by the idea that she just might be able to make a difference, she volunteered along with seventeen others to try to register at the county courthouse in the town of Indianola.

On August 31 the group piled into an old school bus and set off on their historic journey. Upon their arrival in Indianola, Hamer talked to the county clerk about what they wanted to do. The clerk then made them all fill out a long application form. They also had to take a literacy test that required them to read and explain sections of the state constitution.

While they were heading home, the harassment began. Police stopped the bus, claiming its color was "too yellow" and that people might mistake it for a real school bus. The

The Southern Christian Leadership Conference and the Student Nonviolent Coordinating Committee

The Southern Christian Leadership Conference (SCLC) is a civil rights organization founded by Dr. **Martin Luther King, Jr.** (see entry), in 1957. Its goal is to obtain equal rights for blacks and other minorities through nonviolent methods.

Founded in 1960, the Student Nonviolent Coordinating Committee (SNCC) was also a civil rights organization. It recruited members among black and white college students to take part in nonviolent protests against segregation. It broke up in 1969.

Both the SCLC and the SNCC took a leading role in voter registration drives throughout the South during the 1960s. Segregationists had long used a variety of tactics to keep blacks away from the voting booth. Sometimes, they relied on outright threats of violence. In other cases, they turned to literacy requirements and poll taxes to make certain people ineligible to take part in the election process. For example, a would-be black voter in the South could be disqualified if he or she failed a complex "test" that supposedly proved whether a person was smart enough to vote. Other blacks (as well as poor whites) who could not afford to pay a special poll tax were also barred from voting.

driver, who also owned the bus, was fined $100 and ordered to pay up immediately. The riders took up a collection among themselves and managed to come up with about $30, which a local judge accepted as payment. Later, everyone on the bus learned that they had failed the literacy test. (Hamer didn't pass it until her third try in January 1963.)

Hamer had not seen the end of her troubles. Her boss was angry that she had tried to register to vote, so he fired her and ordered her to leave the plantation. A few days later, the house in which she was staying with a friend was sprayed with gunfire. On another occasion, she was shot at from a speeding car. During the months that followed, both Hamer's husband and daughter were arrested and lost their jobs. Police barged into the family home and searched it without a warrant. Even the local water department tried to complicate their lives by sending them a bill for $9,000—despite the fact that they did not have running water!

Hamer stood up to the intimidation and harassment. In fact, the woman who later declared that she was "sick and *tired of being sick and tired" promised never to give up, "even if they shoot me down." Her determination nearly cost her her life in 1963 when she defied a "whites only" policy at a bus terminal in the town of Winona, Mississippi. Arrested and charged with disorderly conduct, she was taken to jail. There guards ordered two black male prisoners to beat her or face severe punishment themselves. They obeyed, and the injuries she received at their hands left her with permanent physical damage.*

Cofounds Mississippi Freedom Democratic Party

Hamer became more determined than ever to resist the system that encouraged such brutality. In 1964, she became involved in politics as cofounder of the Mississippi Freedom Democratic Party (MFDP). It sprang up as an alternative to the so-called "regular" state Democratic Party, an all-white organization that favored keeping segregation laws in the South. The MFDP wanted to challenge the right of the Mississippi Democratic Party to represent the state at that summer's Democratic National Convention in Atlantic City, New Jersey.

On August 22, 1964, the first day of the convention, national Democratic Party officials met to hear the MFDP argue that it deserved to represent the people of Mississippi at the convention, not the "regular" Democrats. An often-tearful Hamer spoke on behalf of the group, giving a simple yet moving account of what she had been forced to endure as a result of her civil rights activities. Her testimony is reprinted here from Proceedings of the Democratic National Convention: 1964—Credentials Committee, Democratic National Committee, 1964.

Mr. Chairman, and the Credentials Committee, my name is Mrs. Fannie Lou Hamer, and I live at 626 East Lafayette Street, Ruleville, Mississippi, Sunflower County, the home of Senator James O. Eastland, and Senator [John] Stennis. [Both Eastland and Stennis were powerful Democratic politicians who opposed integration and blocked civil rights legislation in the U.S. Senate.]

It was the 31st of August in 1962 that eighteen of us traveled twenty-six miles to the county courthouse in Indianola to try to register to try to become first-class citizens.

We was met in Indianola by Mississippi men, Highway Patrolmens, and they only allowed two of us in to take the literacy test at the time. After we had taken this test and started back to Ruleville, we was held up by the City Police and the State Highway Patrolmen and carried back to Indianola where the bus driver was charged that day with driving a bus the wrong color.

After we paid the fine among us, we continued on to Ruleville, and Reverend Jeff Sunny carried me four miles in the rural area where I had worked as a timekeeper and sharecropper for eighteen years. I was met there by my children, who told me the plantation owner was angry because I had gone down to try to register.

After they told me, my husband came, and said the plantation owner was raising Cain because I had tried to register, and before he quit talking the plantation owner came, and said, "Fannie Lou, do you know—did Pap tell you what I said?"

And I said, "Yes, sir."

He said, "I mean that," he said, "If you don't go down and withdraw your registration, you will have to leave," said, "Then if you go down and withdraw," he said, "You will—you might have to go because we're not ready for that in Mississippi."

And I addressed him and told him and said, "I didn't try to register for you. I tried to register for myself."

I had to leave that same night.

On the 10th of September, 1962, sixteen bullets was fired into the home of Mr. and Mrs. Robert Tucker for me. That same night two girls were shot in Ruleville, Mississippi. Also Mr. Joe McDonald's house was shot in.

And in June, the 9th, 1963, I had attended a voter registration workshop, was returning back to Mississippi. Ten of us

Fannie Lou Hamer testifies before Senate, 1965

was traveling by the Continental Trailway bus. When we got to Winona, Mississippi, which is Montgomery County, four of the people got off to use the washroom, and two of the people—to use the restaurant—two of the people wanted to use the washroom.

The four people that had gone in to use the restaurant was ordered out. During this time I was on the bus. But when I looked through the window and saw they had rushed out I got off of the bus to see what had happened, and one of the ladies said, "It was a State Highway Patrolman and a Chief of Police ordered us out."

I got back on the bus and one of the persons had used the washroom got back on the bus, too.

As soon as I was seated on the bus, I saw when they began to get the four people in a highway patrolman's car, [so] I stepped off of the bus to see what was happening and somebody screamed from the car that the four workers was in and said, "Get that one there," and when I went to get in the car, when the man told me I was under arrest, he kicked me.

I was carried to the county jail, and put in the booking room. They left some of the people in the booking room and began to place us in cells. I was placed in a cell with a young woman called Miss Ivesta Simpson. After I was placed in the cell I began to hear sounds of licks and screams. I could hear the sounds of licks and horrible screams, and I could hear somebody say, "Can you say, 'Yes, sir,' nigger?" Can you say, 'Yes, sir?'"

And they would say other horrible names.

She would say, "Yes, I can say, 'Yes, sir.'"

"So, say it."

She says, "I don't know you well enough."

They beat her, I don't know how long, and after a while she began to pray, and asked God to have mercy on those people.

And it wasn't too long before three white men came to my cell. One of these men was a State Highway Patrolman and he asked me where I was from, and I told him Ruleville, [and] he said, "We are going to check this."

And they left my cell and it wasn't too long before they came back. He said, "You are from Ruleville all right," and he used a curse word, and he said, "We are going to make you wish you was dead."

I was carried out of that cell into another cell where they had two Negro prisoners. The State Highway Patrolmen ordered the first Negro to take the **blackjack**.

The first Negro prisoner ordered me, by orders from the State Highway Patrolman for me, to lay down on a bunk bed on my face, and I laid on my face.

The first Negro began to beat, and I was beat by the first Negro until he was exhausted, and I was holding my hands

blackjack: a weapon made from a piece of metal covered with leather that hangs from a hand strap and is used to strike.

Fannie Lou Hamer

behind me at that time on my left side because I suffered from polio when I was six years old.

After the first Negro had beat until he was exhausted the State Highway Patrolman ordered the second Negro to take the blackjack. The second Negro began to beat and I began to work my feet, and the State Highway Patrolman ordered the first Negro who had beat to set on my feet to keep me from working my feet. I began to scream and one white man got up and began to beat me in my head and tell me to hush.

One white man—my dress had worked up high, he walked over and pulled my dress down and he pulled my dress back, back up.

I was in jail when Medgar Evers was murdered.

All of this is on account we want to register, to become first-class citizens, and if the Freedom Democratic Party is not seated now, I question America, is this America, the land of the free and the home of the brave where we have to sleep with our telephones off of the hooks because our lives be threatened daily because we want to live as decent human beings, in America?

Thank you.

99

Hamer's emotional plea—"Is this America?"—deeply touched many of the people who watched news reports of her testimony on national television that evening. As Mamie E. Locke declared in an essay on Hamer published in Women in the Civil Rights Movement, "In that one question, Fannie Lou Hamer ... brought America face to face with itself—its racism, **bigotry,** intolerance, hatred, and **hypocrisy.**"

Members of the MFDP, the "regular" Mississippi Democrats, and the national party were never able to agree on who should be allowed to represent the state at the convention. After the "regular" Mississippi Democrats walked out in protest, the MFDP representatives, led by Hamer, tried to take over their empty seats. Again and again they tried, but they were always escorted out of the hall. They finally left Atlantic City in frustration.

bigotry: prejudice.

hypocrisy: pretending to have high moral standards but not really living by them.

Later that year, Hamer ran unsuccessfully as an MFDP candidate for the U.S. House of Representatives. In 1965, she challenged the election victories of all five of Mississippi's congressmen. She argued that literacy requirements and poll taxes had illegally prevented blacks from voting. After reviewing the evidence, the House rejected her claims.

Despite these and other setbacks, Hamer and the MFDP kept up the political fight in Mississippi with very little help from activists outside the state. At the same time, they had to deal with numerous attempts to discredit them as advocates of race hatred and revolution.

Although the MFDP slowly faded away, it managed to make a lasting impression on national party politics. And Hamer herself became a role model for other poor blacks who had felt abandoned by the system. Strong and seemingly impossible to defeat, she remained a much-loved figure in the civil rights movement. She worked for the SCLC and SNCC as an organizer of welfare and voter registration programs and was also in demand as a speaker.

Hamer died in 1977 after losing a battle to diabetes, heart disease, and breast cancer.

Sources

Books

Crawford, Vicki L., Jacqueline Anne Rouse, and Barbara Woods, *Women in the Civil Rights Movement: Trailblazers and Torchbearers, 1941–1965,* Indiana University Press, 1990.

Lerner, Gerda, editor, *Black Women in White America: A Documentary History,* Pantheon Books, 1972.

Mills, Kay, *This Little Light of Mine: The Life of Fannie Lou Hamer,* Dutton, 1993.

Proceedings of the Democratic National Convention: 1964—Credentials Committee, Democratic National Committee, 1964.

Sewell, George A., *Mississippi History Makers,* University Press of Mississippi, 1977.

Williams, Juan, *Eyes on the Prize: America's Civil Rights Years, 1954-1965,* Viking-Penguin, 1987.

Wright, Nathan, Jr., *What Black Politicians Are Saying,* Hawthorn, 1972.

Periodicals

Ebony, "Black Voices of the South," August 1971, p. 51.

Freedomways, "Life in Mississippi: An Interview with Fannie Lou Hamer," second quarter, spring, 1965, pp. 231-242.

Ms., "The Woman Who Changed the South: A Memory of Fannie Lou Hamer," July 1977, p. 98.

Nation, "'Tired of Being Sick and Tired,'" June 1, 1964, pp. 548-551.

Lorraine Hansberry

1930–1965
Writer and activist

Although she is best remembered as the author of the classic play A Raisin in the Sun, *Lorraine Hansberry was also a social activist with a radical outlook. She fearlessly promoted her causes in print as well as at the microphone, and her outspokenness made her more than a few enemies who would have preferred that she keep quiet. But only an early death silenced the woman who set such an example of what it meant "to be young, gifted and black."*

Early Life

Hansberry was born and raised in an upper-class black neighborhood on the south side of Chicago, Illinois. Her family was well known in the African American community both at a local and a national level for their commitment to the fight for equal rights and racial justice. Thus, Hansberry grew up believing in the value of challenging the status quo (the existing state of affairs). By the time she was in her mid-twenties, she had already decided to combine a life of activism with her desire to write for the stage.

For about two years after she graduated from high school, Hansberry attended the University of Wisconsin. But she soon grew bored and annoyed by classes she felt had no connection to her life and interests. So she dropped out in 1950 and headed to New York City. There Hansberry went to work as a reporter and editor for Freedom, *a radical black newspaper run by prominent singer and activist Paul Robeson. Her 1953 marriage to Robert Nemiroff eventually made it possible for her to quit her job and devote all of her time to creative writing.*

In 1957, Hansberry completed her first (and most famous) play, A Raisin in the Sun. *It dramatizes a black family's struggle against racism and other obstacles as they try to claim their share of the "American Dream" and its promise of a comfortable and prosperous life. Directed by and starring African Americans,* A Raisin in the Sun *opened in New York City in March 1959. It immediately made history as the first play by a black woman ever to run on Broadway.*

Theater critics as well as black and white audiences responded to the realism and drama of A Raisin in the Sun *with tremendous enthusiasm. Hansberry became famous virtually overnight and went on to become the first black playwright (and one of only a few women) to win the prestigious New York Drama Critics Circle award for the best play of the year. Two years later, she enjoyed another round of success upon the release of the film version of* A Raisin in the Sun, *based on a script she herself adapted from her play.*

With the fame Hansberry enjoyed as a celebrated playwright came numerous chances to act on her political views. She supported a variety of causes that were very unpopular at the time. Her concerns ranged from racism and **homophobia** *to* **Pan-Africanism, McCarthyism,** *and global issues of war and peace. Hansberry also had close ties to groups some people considered dangerous to the U.S. government—groups such as the Student Nonviolent Coordinating Committee (SNCC), the Communist party, and various* **black nationalist** *organizations. As a result, she attracted the attention of the FBI.*

homophobia: an unreasonable fear of homosexuals or homosexuality.

Pan-Africanism: the movement for closer ties among all people of African descent.

McCarthyism: a strong anti-communist political attitude in the United States during the 1950s, named after Senator Joseph R. McCarthy.

black nationalist: promoting African Americans' separation from whites to form their own self-governing communities.

Even under the close eye of the FBI, Hansberry did not hesitate to speak out against the U.S. government's excessive interest in the lives of private citizens. On one such occasion, on October 27, 1962, she was invited to address the crowd at a rally in New York City for the abolishment of the House Un-American Activities Committee (HUAC; see box for more information). Her remarks were later published in the winter 1963 issue of Freedomways. *An excerpt from that transcript follows.*

66

I am afraid that I haven't made a speech for a very long time, and there is a significance in that fact which is part of what I should like to talk about this evening.

A week or so ago I was at my typewriter working on a scene in a play of mine in which one character, a German novelist, is trying to explain to another character, an American intellectual, something about what led the greater portion of the German **intelligentsia** to **acquiesce** to Nazism. He says this, "They (the Nazis) permitted us to feel, in return for our silence, that we were non-participants; merely **irrelevant** if inwardly **agonized** observers who had nothing whatsoever to do with that which was being committed in our names."

Just as I put the period after that sentence, my own telephone rang and I was confronted with the voice of Dr. Otto Nathan asking this particular American writer if she would be of this decade and this nation and appear at this rally this evening and join a very necessary **denunciation** of a lingering *American* kind of **travesty.**

It is the sort of moment of truth that dramatists dearly love to put on the stage but find as uncomfortable as everyone else in life. To make it short, however, I am here.

I mean to say that one can become detached in this world of ours…. And then we wake up one day and find that the better people of our nation are still where they were when we last noted them: in the courts defending *our* constitutional rights for us.

intelligentsia: intellectuals who form an artistic, social, or political class of their own.

acquiesce: give in, accept.

irrelevant: not applicable to the situation.

agonized: tormented.

denunciation: criticism, condemnation.

travesty: distorted or inferior imitation of something.

Lorraine Hansberry

The "Red Scare"

From the 1920s until well into the 1950s, the United States was caught in the grip of what was known as the "Red Scare." This was a widespread, almost hysterical fear of **communism** that led to crackdowns on suspected radicals, union activists, foreigners, and anyone else who appeared to be a threat. This fear grew even stronger during the late 1940s, when some people began to declare that communists had worked their way into positions of power in the U.S. government in order to destroy it.

Congress responded by creating two major investigative committees to expose this so-called communist influence. The first was the House Un-American Affairs Committee (HUAC). Established in 1938, HUAC was originally responsible for keeping an eye on foreign spies and Nazi sympathizers during World War II. After the war ended, however, its attention began to shift to reports of disloyalty among government employees.

HUAC's investigations were expanded in the late 1940s and into the 1950s to include labor unions, peace groups, and various other liberal organizations it accused of secretly plotting to overthrow or weaken the government from inside the system. The committee took a particular interest in Hollywood, supposedly the home of numerous writers and performers with communist leanings. The ones who came under suspicion quickly found themselves shut out of the industry and unable to earn a living. Eventually, the **blacklist** spread to include people outside Hollywood who were involved in radio, television, and the theater. Although HUAC became less active during the 1960s, it was not formally abolished until 1975.

A second major committee involved in rooting out alleged communists and other subversives was the Senate Subcommittee on Investigations, headed by Senator Joseph R. McCarthy. He became well known during the early 1950s for making shocking accusations against high-ranking government officials—mostly in the State Department and in the Army—despite the fact that he had little or no proof that they had actually done anything wrong. Eventually, his bullying tactics and questionable "investigations" led to his downfall. He was officially condemned by the Senate in 1954 and quickly faded from the national scene.

This makes me feel that it might be interesting to talk about where our artists are in the contemporary struggles. Some of them, of course, are being heard and felt.... But the vast majority—where are they?

Well, I am afraid that they are primarily where the ruling powers have always wished the artist to be and to stay: in their studios.... I personally consider that part of this detachment is the direct and indirect result of many years of things like the House Committee [HUAC] and concurrent years of

communism: an economic system in which the government (rather than private individuals or companies) owns and controls the means of producing goods, which are then supposed to be shared by everyone equally.

blacklist: a list of people who are not approved of or who are about to be punished for something.

McCarthyism in all its forms. I mean to suggest that the climate of fear, which we were once told ... would bear a bitter harvest in the culture of our civilization, has in fact come to pass....

Among my contemporaries and colleagues in the arts the search for the roots of war, the **exploitation** of man, of poverty and of despair itself, is sought in any arena other than the one which has shaped these artists. Having discovered that the world is **incoherent** they have, some of them, also come to the conclusion that it is also unreal and, in any case, beyond the corrective powers of human energy. Having determined that life is in fact an **absurdity,** they have not yet decided that the task of the thoughtful is to try and help impose purposefulness on that absurdity. They don't yet agree, by and large, that simply being against life as it is is not enough.... In a word, they do not yet agree that it is perhaps the task, I should think certainly the joy, of the artist to chisel out some expression of what life can conceivably be....

I am thinking now, mainly, of course, of writers of my generation. It is they ... who do not yet agree that ... whatever man **renders,** creates, imagines—he can render afresh, re-create and even more gloriously re-imagine. But, I must repeat, that anyone who can even think so these days is held to be an example of **unparalleled** simple mindedness.

Why? For this is what is **cogent** to our meeting tonight; the writers that I am presently thinking of come mainly from my generation. That is to say that they come from a generation which was betrayed in the late forties and fifties by the domination of McCarthyism. We were ceaselessly told, after all, to be everything which **mutilates** youth: to be silent, to be ignorant, to be without **unsanctioned** opinions, to be **compliant** and, above all else, obedient to all the ideas which are in fact the **dregs** of an age....

As for those who went directly into science or industry it was all even less **oblique** than any of that. If you went to the wrong debates on campus, signed the wrong petitions, you simply didn't get the job you wanted, and you were forewarned of this early in your college career.

And, of course, things are a little different than in my parents' times, I mean with regard to the **candor** with which

exploitation: unfair use of another person for one's own profit.

incoherent: lacking order and logic.

absurdity: something ridiculously unreasonable or meaningless.

renders: makes.

unparalleled: unequalled.

cogent: related.

mutilates: cripples.

unsanctioned: unapproved.

compliant: willing to give in to the wishes of others.

dregs: leftovers, the most undesirable part of something.

oblique: indirect, obscure.

candor: honesty, frankness.

Lorraine Hansberry

young people have been made to think in terms of money. It is the only single purpose which has been put before them....

What makes me think of that in connection with what we are speaking of tonight?... If, after all, the ambition in life is merely to be rich, then all which might threaten that possibility is much to be avoided, is it not?

This means, therefore, not incurring the disfavor of employers. It means that one will not protest war if one expects to draw one's livelihood from, say, the aircraft industry if one is an engineer. Or, in the arts, how can one write plays which have either **implicit** or **explicit** in them a quality of the **detestation** of **commerciality** if in fact one is **beholden** to the commerciality of the professional theatre? How can one protest the criminal persecution of political **dissenters** if one has already discovered at nineteen that to do so is to risk a profession?

If all one's morality is wedded to the **opportunist**, the **expedient** in life how can one have the deepest, most profound moral outrage about the fact of the condition of the Negro people in the United States? Particularly ... when one has it **dinned** into one's ears day after day that the only reason why, perhaps, that troublesome and provocative group of people must some day be permitted to buy a cup of coffee or rent an apartment or get a job—is NOT because of the recognition of the universal humanity of the human race but because it happens to be extremely expedient international politics to now think of granting these things!

As I stand here I know perfectly well that such institutions as the House Committee, and all the other little committees, have dragged on their particular obscene **theatrics** for all these years not to expose "communists" or do anything really in connection with the "security" of the United States but merely to create an atmosphere where, in the first place, I should be afraid to come here tonight at all and, secondly, to absolutely guarantee that I will not say what I am going to say, which is this:

I think that my government is wrong. I would like to see them turn back our ships from the Caribbean. The Cuban people, to my mind, and I speak only for myself, have chosen their destiny and I cannot believe that it is the place of

implicit: implied, suggested.

explicit: fully and openly expressed without any doubt as to one's meaning or intent.

detestation: hatred.

commerciality: excessive emphasis on making a profit or appealing to the largest possible number of people.

beholden: under obligation, indebted.

dissenters: protesters.

opportunist: something that can be taken advantage of with little regard for what impact it will have on others.

expedient: something that can bring about immediate advantages with little regard for whether it is right or wrong to do.

dinned: loudly repeated.

theatrics: excessive displays of drama or emotion set up to achieve maximum effect on an audience.

Hansberry at work: "It is perhaps the task, I should think certainly the joy, of the artist to chisel out some expression of what life can conceivably be."

the descendants of those who did not ask the **monarchists** of the eighteenth century for permission to make the United States a republic, to interfere with the twentieth century choice of another sovereign people.

I will go further, speaking as a Negro in America, and impose a little of what Negroes say all the time to each other on what I am saying to you. And that is that it would be a

monarchists: people who support a government run by an absolute ruler (such as a king or queen).

176   Lorraine Hansberry

great thing if they would not only turn back the ships from the Caribbean but turn to the affairs of our country that need righting. For one thing, empty the legislative and judicial chambers of the victims of political persecution so we know why that lamp [the Statue of Liberty] is burning out there in the Brooklyn waters. And, while they are at it, go on and help fulfill the American dream and empty the Southern jails of the genuine heroes, practically the last **vestige** of dignity that we have to boast about at this moment in our history—those students whose imprisonment for trying to insure what is already on the books is our national disgrace at this moment.

And I would go so far, perhaps with an over sense of drama, but I don't think so, to say that maybe without waiting for another two men to die, that we send those troops to finish the Reconstruction in Alabama, Georgia, Mississippi and every place else where the fact of our federal flag flying creates the false notion that what happened at the end of the Civil War was the defeat of the slavocracy at the political as well as the military level. And I say this not merely in behalf of the black and oppressed but, for a change, and more and more thoughtful Negroes must begin to make this point, also for the white and **disinherited** of the South; those poor whites who, by the millions, have been made the tragic and **befuddled** of their own oppression at the hand of the most sinister political **apparatus** in our country. I think perhaps that if our government would do that it would not have to compete in any wishful way for the respect of the new black and brown nations of the world.

Finally, I think that all of us who are thinking about such things, who wish to exercise these rights that we are here defending tonight, must really exercise them. Speaking to my fellow artists in particular, I think that we must paint them, sing them, write about them. All these matters which are not currently fashionable. Otherwise, I think … we are **indulging** in a luxurious **complicity**—and no other thing.

I personally agree with those who say that from here on in, if we are to survive, we, the people—still an excellent phrase—we the people of the world must oblige the heads of all governments to become responsible to us…. I think that it is **imperative** to say "NO" to all of it; no to war of any kind, any where. And I think, therefore, and it is my reason for

vestige: fragment, piece.

disinherited: deprived of human and natural rights.

befuddled instruments: confused people used and abused by others to achieve a certain goal.

apparatus: organization.

indulging: giving in to, taking pleasure in.

complicity: taking part in a wrongful act.

imperative: absolutely necessary.

being here tonight, that it is imperative to remove from the American fabric any and all such institutions or agencies such as the House Committee on Un-American Activities which are designed expressly to keep us from saying—"NO!"

99

Lorraine Hansberry died of cancer on January 12, 1965.

Sources

Books

Foner, Philip S., *The Voice of Black America: Major Speeches by Negroes in the United States, 1797-1971,* Simon & Schuster, 1972.

Hansberry, Lorraine, *To Be Young, Gifted and Black: Lorraine Hansberry in Her Own Words,* edited by Robert Nemiroff, Prentice-Hall, 1969.

Periodicals

Crisis, "Lorraine Hansberry: Portrait of an Angry Young Writer," April 1979, pp. 123-128.

Freedomways, "The Challenge to Artists," winter, 1963, pp. 31-35; "Lorraine Hansberry at the Summit," Number 19, 1979, pp. 269-272.

Washington Post, "Raisin in the Sun's Enduring Passion," November 16, 1986.

Other

Lorraine Hansberry Speaks Out: Art and the Black Revolution (recording), Caedmon, 1972.

Frances Ellen Watkins Harper

1825–1911

Writer, lecturer, abolitionist, and women's rights activist

Frances Ellen Watkins Harper, an extraordinarily talented black woman of the nineteenth century, was a poet, an author of short stories and a novel, and a lecturer. In recognition of her many accomplishments she was nicknamed the "Bronze Muse." (A muse is someone who inspires others to create; the term comes from the muses of Greek mythology, nine sister goddesses who guided and controlled the arts and sciences and were thought to provide inspiration to all artists.) But it was as a lecturer that Harper had her greatest impact, first as an antislavery activist and later as a crusader for women's rights and moral reform.

Early Life

Born of free parents in Baltimore, Maryland, Harper grew up there in the home of an aunt and uncle after being orphaned at an early age. She attended a private school run by her uncle until she was thirteen, at which time she

"A GOVERNMENT WHICH CAN PROTECT AND DEFEND ITS CITIZENS FROM WRONG AND OUTRAGE AND DOES NOT IS VICIOUS."

went to work as a housekeeper for a family that owned a bookstore. Her employer encouraged her to spend her free time reading and writing, and before long the young woman was composing her first poems and essays.

Harper left Maryland in 1850 and taught school for several years in Ohio and Pennsylvania. Around the mid-1850s, she launched her career as an antislavery lecturer. This work required her to travel extensively throughout New England, New York, Ohio, and eastern Canada to deliver as many as three or four speeches in a single day. During this period, Harper also published her first few volumes of poetry. (She eventually produced some ten books of verse that sold well enough to provide her with a modest income.) And in 1859, she became the first African American woman to publish a short story.

Lectures on Conditions in the Reconstruction-Era South

After the Civil War, Harper continued to lecture on behalf of the women's movement and the Women's Christian Temperance Union (temperance is the practice of refusing to drink alcoholic beverages). Her major concern, however, was the issue of racial discrimination and oppression. While on a lengthy speaking tour across the South during the late 1860s and early 1870s, she saw firsthand that former slaves were living under conditions nearly as unbearable as those that had existed before the war. Lynchings and other forms of racial intimidation were widespread. As a result, the lives of many Southern blacks had become desperate. This topic later served as the inspiration for Harper's only novel, Iola Leroy; or Shadows Uplifted. Published in 1892, it was the first book by a black writer to show how African Americans actually lived in the South after the Civil War.

In view of this deplorable state of affairs, Harper—like many of her fellow black activists—came to realize that achieving equal rights for women had to wait until African Americans were guaranteed certain basic freedoms. This was the theme of her speech at a meeting of the National Council of Women held on February 23, 1891. Harper's remarks were originally published in 1891 in Transactions.

They were later reprinted in Black Women in Nineteenth-Century American Life: Their Words, Their Thoughts, Their Feelings, *edited by Bert James Loewenberg and Ruth Bogin, Pennsylvania State University Press, 1976. It is from that book that the following excerpt is taken.*

66

I deem it a privilege to present the negro, not as a mere dependent asking for northern sympathy or southern compassion, but as a member of the body politic who has a claim upon the nation for justice, simple justice, which is the right of every race, upon the government for protection, which is the rightful claim of every citizen, and upon our common Christianity for the best influences which can be exerted for peace on earth and goodwill to man.

Our first claim upon the nation and government is the claim for protection to human life. That claim should lie at the basis of our civilization, not simply in theory but in fact. Outside of America, I know of no other civilized country ... where men are still lynched, murdered, and even burned for real or supposed crimes. As long as there are such cases as moral irresponsibility, mental imbecility; as long as Potiphar's wife stands in the world's **pillory** of shame, no man should be deprived of life or liberty without due process of law. [Potiphar's wife was a woman in the Bible who falsely accused Joseph of trying to seduce her when she had actually tried to seduce him. He was then imprisoned as a result of her charges.]

A government which has power to tax a man in peace, and draft him in war, should have power to defend his life in the hour of peril. A government which can protect and defend its citizens from wrong and outrage and does not is vicious. A government which would do it and cannot is weak; and where human life is insecure through either weakness or viciousness in the administration of law, there must be a lack of justice, and where this is wanting nothing can make up the deficiency.

The strongest nation on earth cannot afford to deal unjustly towards its weakest and feeblest members. A man

body politic: a group of people who are politically organized under a single government.

pillory: a wooden frame with three holes into which a person puts his head and his hands to submit to public punishment for committing a crime.

unscathed: unharmed.

asunder: apart.

cohesion: unity.

chaff: the seed covering and other material separated from grain when it is harvested—in other words, something fairly worthless.

might just as well attempt to play with the thunderbolts of heaven and expect to escape **unscathed,** as for a nation to trample on justice and right and evade the divine penalty. The reason our nation snapped **asunder** in 1861 was because it lacked the **cohesion** of justice; men poured out their blood like water, scattered their wealth like **chaff,** summoned to the field the largest armies the nation had ever seen, but they did not get their final victories which closed the rebellion till they clasped hands with the negro, and marched with him abreast to freedom and to victory.

I claim for the negro protection in every right with which the government has invested him. Whether it was wise or unwise, the government has exchanged the **fetters** on his wrist for the ballot in his right hand, and men cannot **vitiate** his vote by **fraud,** or **intimidate** the voter by violence, without being untrue to the genius and spirit of our government, and bringing **demoralization** into their own political life and ranks.

Am I here met with the objection that the negro is poor and ignorant, and the greatest amount of land, capital, and intelligence is possessed by the white race, and that in a number of states negro **suffrage** means negro supremacy? But is it not a fact that both North and South power naturally **gravitates** into the strongest hands, and is there any danger that a race who were deemed so inferior as to be only fitted for slavery, and social and political **ostracism,** has in less than one generation become so powerful that, if not **hindered** from exercising the right of suffrage, it will dominate over a people who have behind them ages of **dominion,** education, freedom, and civilization, a people who have had poured into their veins the blood of some of the strongest races on earth?

More than a year since [Southern journalist and orator] Mr. [Henry] Grady said, I believe, "We do not directly fear the political **domination** of blacks, but that they are ignorant and easily **deluded,** impulsive and therefore easily led, strong of race instinct and therefore **clannish,** without information and therefore without political **convictions,** passionate and therefore easily excited, poor, irresponsible, and with no idea of the **integrity** of suffrage and therefore easily bought. The fear is that this vast swarm, ignorant, purchasable, will be impacted and controlled by desperate and **unscrupulous** white men and made to hold the balance of power when white men are divided." Admit for one moment that every word here is true, and that the whole race should be judged by its worst, and not its best members, does any civilized country legislate to punish a man before he commits a crime?

fetters: chains, shackles.

vitiate: weaken, make ineffective.

fraud: cheating, deception, trickery.

intimidate: frighten or threaten.

demoralization: disorder, discouragement.

suffrage: right to vote.

gravitates: moves toward, becomes attracted to.

ostracism: exclusion, rejection.

hindered: prevented.

dominion: control, authority.

domination: supremacy.

deluded: tricked.

clannish: inclined to associate only with members of one's own group.

convictions: beliefs.

integrity: honesty, purity.

unscrupulous: corrupt.

It is said the negro is ignorant. But why is he ignorant? It comes with ill grace from a man who has put out my eyes to make a parade of my blindness—to **reproach** me for my poverty when he has **wronged me of** my money. If the negro is ignorant, he has lived under the shadow of an institution which, at least in part of the country, made it a crime to teach him to read the name of the ever-blessed Christ. If he is poor, what has become of the money he has been earning for the last two hundred and fifty years? Years ago it was said cotton fights and cotton conquers for American slavery. The negro helped build up that great cotton power in the South, and in the North his sigh was in the whir of its machinery, and his blood and tears upon the **warp and woof** of its manufactures.

But there are some rights more precious than the rights of property or the claims of superior intelligence: they are the rights of life and liberty, and to these the poorest and humblest man has just as much right as the richest and most influential man in the country. Ignorance and poverty are conditions which men outgrow. Since the sealed volume was opened by the crimson hand of war, in spite of **entailed** ignorance, poverty, opposition, and a heritage of scorn, schools have sprung like wells in the desert dust. It has been estimated that about two millions have learned to read. Colored men and women have gone into journalism. Some of the finest magazines in the country have received contributions from them. Learned professions have given them diplomas. Universities have granted them professorships. Colored women have combined to shelter orphaned children. Tens of thousands have been contributed by colored persons for the care of the aged and infirm.... Millions of dollars have flowed into the pockets of the race, and freed people have not only been able to provide for themselves, but reach out their hands to impoverished others.

Has the record of the slave been such as to warrant the belief that permitting him to share citizenship with others in the country is **inimical** to the welfare of the nation? Can it be said that he lacks patriotism, or a readiness to make common cause with the nation in the hour of peril? In the days of the American Revolution some of the first blood which was shed flowed from the veins of a colored man [Crispus

reproach: criticize, condemn.

wronged me of: cheated me out of.

warp and woof: foundation, base.

entailed: imposed, forced.

inimical: hostile.

Attucks].... In or after 1812 they [black soldiers] received from General [Andrew] Jackson the **plaudit,** "I knew you would endure hunger and thirst and all the hardships of war. I knew that you loved the land of your **nativity,** and that, like ourselves, you had to defend all that is most dear; but you have surpassed my hopes. I have found in you, united to all these qualities, that noble enthusiasm which **impels** to great deeds." And in our late civil conflict colored men threw their lives into the struggle, rallied around the old flag when others were trampling it underfoot and riddling it with bullets. Colored people learned to regard that flag as a **harbinger** of freedom and bring their most reliable information to the Union army, to share their humble fare with the escaping prisoner; to be faithful when others were faithless and help turn the tide of battle in favor of the nation. While nearly two hundred thousand joined the Union army, others remained on the old plantation; widows, wives, aged men, and helpless children were left behind, when the master was at the front trying to put new rivets in their chains, and yet was there a single slave who took advantage of the master's absence to invade the privacy of his home, or **wreak** a **summary** vengeance on those whose "defenceless condition should have been their best defence?"

Instead of taking the ballot from his hands, teach him how to use it, and to add his **quota** to the progress, strength, and durability of the nation. Let the nation, which once consented to his **abasement** under a system which made it a crime to teach him to read his Bible, feel it a privilege as well as a duty to reverse the old processes of the past by **supplanting** his darkness with light, not simply by providing the negro, but the whole region in which he lives, with national education. No child can be blamed because he was born in the midst of **squalor,** poverty, and ignorance, but society is criminal if it permits him to grow up without proper efforts for **ameliorating** his condition.

Some months since, when I was in South Carolina, where I addressed a number of colored schools, I was informed that white children were in the factories, beginning from eight to ten years old, with working hours from six to seven o'clock; and one day, as a number of white children were **wending** their way apparently from the factory, I heard a colored man

plaudit: praise.
nativity: birth.
impels: drives on, forces.
harbinger: sign, omen.
wreak: cause.
summary: quick and without any formality.
quota: part, share.
abasement: moral or intellectual decay, humiliation.
supplanting: replacing.
squalor: filth.
ameliorating: improving.
wending: traveling.

say, "I pity these children." It was a strange turning of the tables to hear a colored man in South Carolina **bestowing** pity on white children because of neglect in their education. Surely the world does move. When parents are too poor or selfish to spare the labor of their children from the factories, and the state too **indifferent** or short-sighted to enforce their education by law, then let the government save its future citizens from the results of **cupidity** in the parents or short-sightedness in the state.

If today there is danger from a mass of ignorance voting, may there not be a danger even greater, and that is a mass of "ignorance that does not vote"? If there is danger that an ignorant mass might be compacted to hold the balance of power where white men are divided politically, might not that same mass, if kept ignorant and **disfranchised,** be used by wicked men, whose weapons may be bombs and dynamite, to dash themselves against the peace and order of society? Today the hands of the negro are not dripping with dynamite. We do not read of his flaunting the red banners of **anarchy** in the face of the nation, nor plotting in beer-saloons to overthrow existing institutions, nor spitting on the American flag. Once that flag was to him an **ensign** of freedom. Let our government resolve that as far as that flag extends every American-born child shall be able to read upon its folds liberty for all and chains for none.

And now permit me to make my final claim, and that is a claim upon our common Christianity.... It is the pride of Caste which opposes the spirit of Christ, and the great work to which American Christianity is called is a work of Christly reconciliation. God has heaved up your mountains with grandeur, flooded your rivers with majesty, crowned your **vales** with fertility, and enriched your mines with wealth.... Be reconciled to God for making a man black, permitting him to become part of your body politic, and sharing one **rood** or acre of our goodly heritage. Be reconciled to the Christ of Calvary, who said, "And I, if I be lifted up, will draw all men to me," and "It is better for a man that a millstone were hanged about his neck, and he were drowned in the depths of the sea, than that he should offend one of these little ones that believe in me...."

What I ask of American Christianity is not to show us more **creeds,** but more of Christ; not more rites and cere-

bestowing: granting.

indifferent: uninterested, unconcerned.

cupidity: greed.

disfranchised: denied the right to vote.

anarchy: lawlessness, political disorder.

ensign: emblem, banner.

vales: valleys.

rood: a fraction of an acre.

creeds: beliefs, doctrines.

Frances Ellen Watkins Harper

monies, but more religion glowing with love and **replete** with life—religion which will be to all weaker races an uplifting power, and not a **degrading** influence. Jesus Christ has given us a platform of love and duty from which all **oppression** and selfishness is necessarily excluded. While politicians may stumble on the barren mountains of fretful controversy and ask in strange bewilderment, "What shall we do with weaker races?" I hold that Jesus Christ answered that question nearly two thousand years since. "Whatsoever ye would that men should do to you, do you even so to them."

99

Harper continued to write and lecture throughout the 1890s and into the early 1900s. Temperance and women's rights—especially black women's rights—were her main concerns. She died at the age of eighty-seven in 1911.

Sources

Books

Anderson, Judith, *Outspoken Women: Speeches by American Women Reformers, 1635–1935,* Kendall/Hunt, 1984.

Foner, Philip S., editor, *The Voice of Black America: Major Speeches by Negroes in the United States, 1797–1971,* Simon & Schuster, 1972.

Lerner, Gerda, editor, *Black Women in White America: A Documentary History,* Pantheon Books, 1972.

Loewenberg, Bert James, and Ruth Bogin, editors, *Black Women in Nineteenth-Century American Life: Their Words, Their Thoughts, Their Feelings,* Pennsylvania State University Press, 1976.

Sewall, May Wright, editor, *The World's Congress of Representative Women,* Rand, McNally, 1894.

replete: full, overflowing.
degrading: corrupting.
oppression: unjust or cruel use of power and authority.

Barbara Jordan

1936–1996

Politician and educator

Barbara Jordan became a national political figure at a time in American history when many people were thoroughly disillusioned by the conduct of government leaders. Her solemn dignity and unshakable moral convictions were very appealing in the wake of the latest Washington scandal. In addition, her exceptionally deep, powerful voice and precise manner of speaking carried a ring of authority few could ever hope to match. As newspaper columnist Molly Ivins once noted about her longtime friend and fellow Texan: "Her great baritone voice was so impressive that her colleagues ... used to joke that if Hollywood ever needed someone to be the voice of the Lord Almighty, only Jordan would do."

Early Life

A native of Houston, Texas, Jordan was the youngest of three daughters in a poor family headed by a Baptist minister and his wife. Both of her parents expected her to work hard and do well in school, and she grew up with a fierce determination to be the best.

One of the areas in which Jordan showed early promise was public speaking. She first displayed her skills as a member of her high school debate team. She continued to improve her technique in college, graduating from Texas Southern University with a degree in political science and honors in debating. From there, she went on to Boston University and obtained a law degree in 1959. Jordan then returned to Houston and began to practice law from the dining room of her parents' house. Eventually, she was able to save enough money to open up a real office in partnership with another lawyer.

Jordan entered politics during the 1960 presidential race working behind the scenes for the local branch of the Democratic party. She decided to take on a more public role after successfully filling in for a speaker who wasn't able to make a scheduled appearance at a campaign rally. In 1962 and again in 1964, Jordan ran for the Texas House of Representatives but lost both times. In 1966, however, she won a seat in the Texas State Senate. Her victory made her the first black since Reconstruction and the first black woman ever to serve in that particular legislative body. Jordan was re-elected in 1968, then ran for the U.S. Congress in 1972 and easily beat her opponent.

Addresses a National Audience During Nixon Impeachment Hearings

The rookie congresswoman first captured national attention as a member of the U.S. House Judiciary Committee. Since the fall of 1973, the committee had been investigating the Watergate break-in and cover-up (see box). By mid-1974, hearings were under way to consider whether President Richard Nixon should be impeached (formally charged with misconduct while holding public office) for his role in the political scandal. As the time grew near to make a decision, each of the thirty-eight members of the committee was given fifteen minutes to deliver a statement outlining his or her views.

The Watergate Scandal

In June 1972, five men were arrested for breaking into the national headquarters of the Democratic party. The headquarters were located in an apartment and office complex in Washington, D.C., called the Watergate. An investigation showed that the men had been hired by the committee running the re-election campaign of Republican President Richard Nixon.

During the trial of the five burglars, information surfaced indicating that various people in the White House (including the president himself) had known of the break-in before it happened and had later tried to cover it up. Then a series of articles appearing in the *Washington Post* raised even more questions about the entire incident. These revelations eventually led the U.S. Senate to conduct hearings into the widening political scandal that was often referred to simply as "Watergate."

During the course of the Watergate investigation, other illegal activities of the Nixon administration also came to light. For example, aides to the president occasionally tried to discredit his political rivals by obtaining damaging personal information they then "leaked" to the press. (If they couldn't find what they wanted, they would even go so far as to make up something.) They also granted special treatment to individuals and corporations in exchange for big donations to the Republican party.

President Nixon insisted throughout the hearings that he did not know anything about the Watergate break-in before it hap-pened or about the attempts to cover it up. But time and time again, he refused to make public important documents and tapes concerning the affair. Finally, on July 24, 1974, the U.S. Supreme Court ordered the president to cooperate with Senate Watergate committee members and turn over secret tape recordings of certain White House conversations about the break-in. These conversations between Nixon and his top assistants proved that the president not only *knew* about efforts to cover up the illegal activities of the Watergate burglars, he had actually *ordered* the cover-up.

Meanwhile, members of the House Judiciary Committee—including Barbara Jordan—had been debating since May 1974 whether President Nixon should be impeached. By July 30, they had voted to charge him with three offenses that could have resulted in his removal from office: taking part in a criminal conspiracy to obstruct justice, abusing his powers as president, and refusing to cooperate with requests for information. Committee members then passed these recommendations along to the full House of Representatives for further consideration.

On August 9, 1974, however, President Nixon chose to resign to spare himself and the country the ordeal of an impeachment hearing. The following month, the new president, Gerald Ford, pardoned Nixon for any crimes he might have committed while serving as president. The decision was extremely controversial because it guaranteed that the former president would never have to face any federal charges.

Jordan's turn to speak came on the evening of July 25. In front of a television audience that numbered in the millions, she made her case for impeachment with a riveting summary of the charges against the president and how those actions had violated the U.S. Constitution. "My faith in the Constitution is whole, it is complete, it is total," she declared. "I am not going to sit here and be an idle spectator to the diminution, the subversion, the destruction of the Constitution.... If the impeachment provision in the Constitution of the United States will not reach the offenses charged here, then perhaps that eighteenth-century Constitution should be abandoned to a twentieth-century paper shredder...."

Two years later, the memory of Jordan's stunning performance before a national television audience was still fresh in the minds of her fellow Democrats. So they invited her to deliver one of two keynote addresses (the opening speech that introduces the issues to be considered) at the 1976 Democratic National Convention in New York City. It was the first time a black woman had ever been chosen for this honor.

The convention had been a rather lifeless affair until Jordan stepped up to the microphone on the evening of July 12. But as her booming voice filled the auditorium, everyone sat up and took notice—delegates and television viewers alike. Her rousing speech was frequently interrupted with cheers and applause. By the next day, there was a serious effort under way to nominate her for vice-president. The following excerpt from Jordan's keynote address is reprinted here from Representative American Speeches: 1976-1977, *edited by Waldo W. Braden, Wilson, 1977.*

One hundred and forty-four years ago [1832], members of the Democratic party first met in convention to select a presidential candidate. Since that time, Democrats have continued to **convene** once every four years and draft a party **platform** and nominate a presidential candidate. And our meeting this week is a continuation of that tradition.

convene: meet.

platform: a declaration of the principles for which a person or a political party stands.

But there is something different about tonight. There is something special about tonight. What is different? What is special? I, Barbara Jordan, am a keynote speaker.

A lot of years passed since 1832, and during that time it would have been most unusual for any national political party to ask that a Barbara Jordan deliver a keynote address ... but tonight here I am. And I feel that notwithstanding the past that my presence here is one additional bit of evidence that the American Dream need not forever be deferred.

Now that I have this grand distinction what in the world am I supposed to say?

I could easily spend this time praising the accomplishments of this party and attacking the Republicans but I don't choose to do that.

I could list the many problems which Americans have. I could list the problems which cause people to feel **cynical,** angry, frustrated: problems which include lack of **integrity** in government; the feeling that the individual no longer counts; the reality of material and spiritual poverty; the feeling that the grand American experiment is failing or has failed. I could recite these problems and then I could sit down and offer no solutions. But I don't choose to do that either.

The citizens of America expect more. They deserve and they want more than a recital of problems.

We are a people in a **quandary** about the present. We are a people in search of our future. We are a people in search of a national community.

We are a people trying not only to solve the problems of the present ... but we are attempting on a larger scale to fulfill the promise of America. We are attempting to fulfill our national purpose; to create and **sustain** a society in which all of us are equal.

Throughout our history, when people have looked for new ways to solve their problems, and to uphold the principles of this nation, many times they have turned to political parties. They have often turned to the Democratic party.

What is it, what is it about the Democratic party that makes it the instrument that people use when they search for

cynical: distrustful of human nature and motives.

integrity: honesty, firm belief in following high moral standards.

quandary: a state of confusion or doubt.

sustain: support, maintain.

Barbara Jordan

ways to shape their future? Well, I believe the answer to that question lies in our concept of governing. Our concept of governing is derived from our view of people. It is a concept deeply rooted in a set of beliefs firmly etched in the national conscience....

First, we believe in equality for all and privileges for none. This is a belief that each American regardless of background has equal standing in the public forum, all of us. Because we believe this idea so firmly, we are an inclusive rather than an exclusive party. Let everybody come....

We believe that the people are the source of all governmental power; that the authority of the people is to be extended, not restricted. This can be accomplished only by providing each citizen with every opportunity to participate in the management of the government....

We believe that the government which represents the authority of all the people, not just one interest group, but all the people, has an obligation to actively underscore, actively seek to remove those obstacles which would block individual achievement ... obstacles emanating from race, sex, economic condition....

We are a party of innovation. We do not reject our traditions, but we are willing to adapt to changing circumstances, when change we must. We are willing to suffer the discomfort of change in order to achieve a better future.

We have a positive vision of the future founded on the belief that the gap between the promise and reality of America can one day be finally closed. We believe that.

This, my friends, is the bedrock of our concept of governing. This is a part of the reason why Americans have turned to the Democratic party. These are the foundations upon which a national community can be built.

Let's all understand that these guiding principles cannot be discarded for short-term political gains. They represent what this country is all about. They are **indigenous** to the American idea. And these are principles which are not **negotiable.**

In other times, I could stand here and give this kind of exposition on the beliefs of the Democratic party and that

indigenous: inborn.

negotiable: subject to being given away or traded in exchange for something else.

would be enough. But today that is not enough. People want more. That is not sufficient reason for the majority of the people of this country to vote Democratic. We have made mistakes. In our haste to do all things for all people, we did not foresee the full consequences of our actions. And when the people raised their voices, we didn't hear. But our deafness was only a temporary condition....

Even as I stand here and admit that we have made mistakes I still believe that as the people of America sit in judgment on each party, they will recognize that our mistakes were mistakes of the heart. They'll recognize that.

And now we must look to the future. Let us heed the voice of the people and recognize their common sense. If we do not, we not only **blaspheme** our political heritage, we ignore the common ties that bind all Americans.

Many fear the future. Many are distrustful of their leaders, and believe that their voices are never heard. Many seek only to satisfy their private work wants. To satisfy private interests.

But this is the great danger America faces. That we will cease to be one nation and become instead a collection of interest groups; city against suburb, region against region, individual against individual....

If that happens, who then will speak for America?

Who then will speak for the common good?

This is the question which must be answered in 1976.

Are we to be one people bound together by common spirit sharing in a common endeavor or will we become a divided nation?

For all of its uncertainty, we cannot flee the future. We must not become the new **puritans** and reject our society. We must address and master the future together. It can be done if we restore the belief that we share a sense of national community, that we share a common national endeavor. It can be done....

As a first step, we must restore our belief in ourselves. We are a generous people, so why can't we be generous with each other? We need to take to heart the words spoken by Thomas Jefferson: "Let us restore to social intercourse that harmony

blaspheme: to speak of something sacred without proper respect or seriousness.

puritans: people who practice or preach a very strict moral code.

Barbara Jordan's powerful voice and precise way of speaking were well known and respected by colleagues and audiences

and that affection without which liberty and even life are but dreary things."

A nation is formed by the willingness of each of us to share in the responsibility for upholding the common good.

A government is **invigorated** when each of us is willing to participate in shaping the future of this nation.

invigorated: made livelier and more energetic.

In this election year we must define the common good and begin again to shape a common good and begin again to shape a common future. Let each person do his or her part. If one citizen is unwilling to participate, all of us are going to suffer. For the American idea, though it is shared by all of us, is realized in each one of us.

And now, what are those of us who are elected public officials supposed to do? We call ourselves public servants but I'll tell you this: we as public servants must set an example for the rest of the nation. It is **hypocritical** for the public official to **admonish** and **exhort** the people to uphold the common good if we are **derelict** in upholding the common good. More is required of public officials than slogans and handshakes and press releases. More is required. We must hold ourselves strictly accountable. We must provide the people with a vision of the future.

If we promise as public officials, we must deliver. If we as public officials propose, we must produce. If we say to the American people it is time for you to be sacrificial; sacrifice.... And again, if we make mistakes, we must be willing to admit them. We have to do that. What we have to do is strike a balance between the idea that government should do everything and the idea ... that government ought to do nothing....

Let there be no illusions about the difficulty of forming this kind of a national community. It's tough.... But a spirit of harmony will survive in America only if each of us remembers that we share a common destiny. If each of us remembers when self-interest and bitterness seem to prevail, that we share a common destiny.

I have confidence that we can form this kind of national community.

I have confidence that the Democratic party can lead the way. I have that confidence. We cannot improve on the system of government handed down to us by the founders of the Republic.... But what we can do is to find new ways to implement that system and realize our destiny.

Now, I began this speech by commenting to you on the uniqueness of a Barbara Jordan making the keynote address. Well, I am going to close my speech by quoting a Republican president, and I ask you that as you listen to these words of

hypocritical: characterized by the practice of pretending to have high moral standards but not really living by them.

admonish: scold.

exhort: urge.

derelict: careless, neglectful.

Abraham Lincoln, relate them to the concept of a national community in which every last one of us participates: "As I would not be a slave, so I would not be a master."

This expresses my idea of democracy. Whatever differs from this, to the extent of the difference is no democracy.

" "

*In 1977, Jordan announced that she would not run for re-election to Congress in 1978. She did not retire from public life, however. At the end of her term, she joined the faculty of the Lyndon B. Johnson School of Public Affairs at the University of Texas in Austin. She also served as an advisor on **ethics** to former Texas Governor Ann Richards and was chair of the independent U.S. Commission on Immigration Reform. And she continued to fulfill numerous speaking engagements, including delivering the keynote address at the 1992 Democratic National Convention.*

Around the time she decided to leave Congress, Jordan was diagnosed with multiple sclerosis, a neurological (having to do with the nerves, the brain, or the spinal cord) disease characterized by muscle tremors and partial or complete paralysis. It eventually left her dependent on a wheelchair or a walker.

Jordan died of pneumonia in January 1996. It was believed to be a complication of leukemia, from which she had been suffering for about a year.

Sources

Books

Blue, Rose, and Corinne Naden, *Barbara Jordan,* Chelsea House, 1992.

Braden, Waldo W., editor, *Representative American Speeches: 1974–1975,* Wilson, 1975.

Braden, Waldo W., editor, *Representative American Speeches: 1976–1977,* Wilson, 1977.

Debate on Articles of Impeachment: Hearings of the Committee on the Judiciary, House of Representatives, 93rd Congress, 2nd Session, U.S. Government Printing Office, 1974.

ethics: moral principles and values.

Duffy, Bernard K., and Halford R. Ryan, editors, *American Orators of the Twentieth Century: Critical Studies and Sources,* Greenwood Press, 1987.

Haskins, James, *Barbara Jordan,* Dial Press, 1977.

Jordan, Barbara, and Shelby Hearon, *Barbara Jordan: A Self-Portrait,* Doubleday, 1979.

Kennedy, Patricia Scileppi, and Gloria Hartman O'Shields, *We Shall Be Heard: Women Speakers in America, 1828–Present,* Kendall/Hunt, 1983.

Roberts, Naurice, *Barbara Jordan: The Great Lady from Texas,* Childrens Press, 1984.

Periodicals

Chicago Tribune, "A Powerful Voice of Nation, Barbara Jordan, Dies," January 17, 1996; "Ex-U.S. Rep. Barbara Jordan Dies," January 18, 1996.

Detroit News, "Ex-Congresswoman 'Was…a Source of Inspiration' to Many," January 18, 1996, p. 2A.

New York Times, "Black Woman Keynoter: Barbara Charline Jordan," July 13, 1976, p. 24; January 18, 1996 (obituary).

Index

Bolds indicate featured speakers and volume numbers; illustrations are marked (ill.).

Slave uprisings I:131

Slavocracy I:177

Social equality II:361

Socialism I:41; II:244

SOSAD (Save Our Sons and Daughters) II:305

Soul on Ice I:65

The Souls of Black Folk I:102

Southern Christian Leadership Conference (SCLC) I:161, 162, 168; II:206, 241

Southern Democrats I:13

Southern Horrors II:367

Southern state constitutions I:13, 14

Southern states I:14

Spelman College I:114

Stand for Children march I:123

State constitutional conventions I:15; II:348

Stewart, Maria W. Miller II:307-314

Strikes II:273

Student Nonviolent Coordinating Committee (SNCC) I:32, 33, 35, 37, 38, 70, 161, 162, 168, 171; II:207

Student radicalism I:69

Substance abuse I:71-72, 115

Summer of 1967 I:61

T

Teachers I:105

Technical training I:105

Technology I:47

Teenage pregnancy I:115, 117

Temperance I:180; II:336

Temple of Islam II:229

Terrell, Mary Church II:315-321, 315 (ill.)

Texas State Senate I:189

Thirteenth Amendment I:135

Thomas and Beulah I:88, 93-96

Thomas, Clarence II:259, 322-334, 322 (ill.), 329 (ill.)

369th Infantry Regiment I:142

Thurmond, Strom II:233, 261

Total Recall II:304

Touré, Kwame I:31, 41

Trade unions I:6, 9; II:214, 320, 390

Truth, Sojourner II:335-345, 339 (ill.), 343 (ill.)

Turner, Henry McNeal II:346-354, 346 (ill.)

Turner, Nat I:131

Tuskegee Airmen II:292

Tuskegee Institute I:104; II:356, 362 (ill.)

U

United Daughters of the Confederacy II:261, 262, 264

United Nations I:21, 23-4, 29

United States Military Academy at West Point II:291

Universal Negro Improvement Association (UNIA) I:136-144,

Urban League I:142; II:407

U.S. Army
racial discrimination II:291

U.S. Commission on Immigration Reform I:197

U.S. Congress I:11, 13, 55

U.S. Constitution I:16-17, 191; II:208, 248, 250, 252, 270, 387
on slavery I:82-83

U.S. House of Representatives II:273, 280-281

U.S. Senate I:11-13; II:258-261

U.S. Supreme Court II:247, 249, 255, 322, 330, 333

V

Vandercook, John I:4

Vesey, Denmark I:131

Veterans of World War I I:136

Vietnam Veterans Memorial (ill.) II:287

Vietnam war I:56-62; II:214

Violence I:115, 116-119, 122; II:297, 299, 304
and television I:117
and the movies I:117; II:304

Violence prevention II:298-300

Vocational training programs I:3, 4

Voter intimidation I:13, 160-169, 183

Voter registration drives I:114, 160, 161, 162, 164, 168; II:206, 212

Voting fraud I:13, 15, 183; II:385, 387

Voting laws I:161

Voting power II:236

Voting rights I:13, 16, 19, 160-169, 185, 186; II:213, 232, 233, 236, 251, 341, 342, 385, 387
literacy tests I:162
poll taxes I:162

W

Walcott, Louis Eugene. *See Farrakhan, Louis*

Wallace, George II:262

Washington, Booker T. I:4, 101, 110, 136; II:348, **355-364**, 355 (ill.), 359 (ill.)

Washington D.C. II:317, 321

Washington Post I:190

Washington Research Project I:114

Watergate I:189, 190

Watts disturbance II:399

Weapons II:242

Wells-Barnett, Ida B. I:110, II:**365-381**, 365 (ill.), 369 (ill.)

White civil rights activists I:37-38

White, George H. II:382-392, 382 (ill.)

White-league organizations I:15

White racism I:61, 114

White radical movement I:41, 70

Whitesboro, New Jersey II:392

White supremacy I:34, 35